DOMESTIC SPACE IN CL

MW00581350

Housing is shaped by culturally specific expectations about the kinds of architecture and furnishings that are appropriate; about how and where different activities should be carried out; and by and with whom. It is those expectations, and the wider social and cultural systems of which they are a part, that are explored in this volume. At the same time, the book as a whole argues two larger points: first, that while houses, households and families have in recent years become increasingly important as objects of inquiry in Greek and Roman contexts, their potential as sources of information about broader social-historical issues has yet to be fully realised; and second, that greater weight and independence should be given to material culture as a source for studying ancient history. The book will be invaluable to upper-level undergraduates, graduate students and scholars.

LISA C. NEVETT is Associate Professor of Greek Archaeology at the University of Michigan. She has contributed articles and chapters to a wide variety of journals and edited volumes, and her own books include *House and Society in the Ancient Greek World* (Cambridge, 1999) and *Ancient Greek Houses and Households* (edited with Bradley A. Ault, 2005).

KEY THEMES IN ANCIENT HISTORY

EDITORS

P. A. Cartledge
Clare College, Cambridge
P. D. A. Garnsey
Jesus College, Cambridge

Key Themes in Ancient History aims to provide readable, informed and original studies of various basic topics, designed in the first instance for students and teachers of Classics and ancient history, but also for those engaged in related disciplines. Each volume is devoted to a general theme in Greek, Roman or, where appropriate, Graeco-Roman history, or to some salient aspect or aspects of it. Besides indicating the state of current research in the relevant area, authors seek to show how the theme is significant for our own as well as ancient culture and society. By providing books for courses that are oriented around themes it is hoped to encourage and stimulate promising new developments in teaching and research in ancient history.

Other books in the series

Death-ritual and social structure in classical antiquity, by Ian Morris
978 0 521 37465 1 (hardback) 978 0 521 37611 2 (paperback)

Literacy and orality in ancient Greece, by Rosalind Thomas
978 0 521 37346 3 (hardback) 978 0 521 37742 3 (paperback)

Slavery and society at Rome, by Keith Bradley
978 0 521 37287 9 (hardback) 978 0 521 37887 1 (paperback)

Law, violence, and community in classical Athens, by David Cohen
978 0 521 38167 3 (hardback) 978 0 521 38837 5 (paperback)

Public order in ancient Rome, by Wilfried Nippel
978 0 521 38327 1 (hardback) 978 0 521 38749 1 (paperback)

Friendship in the classical world, by David Konstan
978 0 521 45402 5 (hardback) 978 0 521 45998 3 (paperback)

Sport and society in ancient Greece, by Mark Golden
978 0 521 49698 8 (hardback) 978 0 521 49790 9 (paperback)

Food and society in classical antiquity, by Peter Garnsey
978 0 521 64182 1 (hardback) 978 0 521 64588 1 (paperback)

DOMESTIC SPACE
IN CLASSICAL ANTIQUITY

LISA C. NEVETT

CAMBRIDGE
UNIVERSITY PRESS

CAMBRIDGE UNIVERSITY PRESS
Cambridge, New York, Melbourne, Madrid, Cape Town, Singapore,
São Paulo, Delhi, Dubai, Tokyo, Mexico City

Cambridge University Press
The Edinburgh Building, Cambridge CB2 8RU, UK

Published in the United States of America by Cambridge University Press, New York

www.cambridge.org
Information on this title: www.cambridge.org/9780521789455

First published 2010

Printed in the United Kingdom at the University Press, Cambridge

A catalogue record for this publication is available from the British Library

Library of Congress Cataloguing in Publication data
Nevett, Lisa C.
Domestic space in classical antiquity / Lisa C. Nevett.
p.   cm. – (Key themes in ancient history)
Includes bibliographical references and index.
ISBN 978-0-521-78336-1 (hardback)
1. Dwellings – Greece – History – To 1500.   2. Dwellings – Rome – History.
3. Households – Greece – History – To 1500.   4. Households – Rome – History.
5. Architecture, Domestic – Greece – History – To 1500.   6. Architecture,
Domestic – Rome – History.   7. Material culture – Greece – History – To 1500.
8. Material culture – Rome – History.   9. Greece – Social conditions – To 146 B.C.
10. Rome – Social conditions.   I. Title.   II. Series.
DF99.N47   2010
392.3′60938 – dc22   2010019224

ISBN 978-0-521-78336-1 Hardback
ISBN 978-0-521-78945-5 Paperback

If the house could speak, it would tell a very clear story
Aeschylus, *Agamemnon* 37–38

The household is a 'sociogram' not of a family but of something much more: of a social system.
Hillier and Hanson 1984, 159

Contents

Figures

x

Plates

Every effort has been made to secure necessary permissions to reproduce other copyright material in this book, though in some cases it has proved impossible to contact copyright holders. If any omissions are brought to our notice, we will be happy to include appropriate acknowledgements in any subsequent edition.

Preface and acknowledgements

For a variety of reasons this volume has taken longer to write than it should have, and I am grateful to the series editors Paul Cartledge and Peter Garnsey, and to Michael Sharp at Cambridge University Press, for patiently awaiting the manuscript. Many of the individual case studies included here represent the result of long engagement with the material on which they are based. In the process, several potential chapters have eventually been excluded and will appear elsewhere. I hope that the sometimes lengthy history of those that remain has helped to make this a better book: I originally presented Chapter 2 as part of a series of seminars on Archaic Greece at Lincoln College, Oxford in 2001 and, in summary form, at a symposium in honour of Anthony Snodgrass held in Cambridge in the same year. Chapter 3 began as a Classical Archaeology seminar paper given in Cambridge in 2001 and a Classical Studies Department seminar paper given at the Open University in 2002; elements of my argument were also presented in summary form at the Annual Meeting of the Archaeological Institute of America in 2005. An overview of the material included in Chapter 4 was given at the meeting of the Classical Association of the Mid-West and South in Madison in 2005. My work on the Pompeian evidence, discussed in Chapter 5, was presented to the Classics Department at the University of Cincinnati in 2006 and to the Archaeology Department at the University of Groningen in the same year. Finally, Chapter 6 represents an expansion of work carried out for a colloquium on Late Antiquity at the Open University in 2000. I thank the organisers and audiences of all of these occasions for their invitations to speak and for their helpful comments and suggestions. In keeping with the conventions of the Key Themes series, since this volume comprises both Greek and Roman topics, the spelling of Greek names has been Latinised (thus the reader will find, for example, 'Olynthus', rather than 'Olynthos'). Translations of the ancient texts are my own unless otherwise stated.

This work could not have been undertaken without the co-operation of a variety of institutions: colleagues at the Open University and, more recently, at the University of Michigan have graciously granted me leave to pursue my research. Funding has been provided by the Arts and Humanities Research Board of Great Britain (Research Leave Award, 2001); the British Academy (Personal Research Grant, 2001); the British School at Rome (Hugh Last Fellowship, 2001); and the Department of Classics, University of Cincinnati (Margo Tytus Visiting Fellowship, 2006). Research funds from the Departments of Classical Studies and the History of Art at Michigan have assisted with some of the plates and figures. I have also been fortunate to benefit from the use of a number of research libraries, including the Classics Faculty and University libraries at the University of Cambridge; and the libraries of the British School at Rome, the British School at Athens, the University of Michigan, the Department of Classics at the University of Cincinnati, and the Strozier Library at Florida State University. I am grateful to the Trustees of the British Museum for permission to use Plates 3.2 and 3.3, to the Kelsey Museum (University of Michigan) for Plates 1.1 and 1.2, to Katherine Dunbabin for Plate 6.1 and to George Braziller Inc. for Plates 6.2, 6.4 and 6.5a.

Most of all, I owe much to the support and advice of friends and colleagues whom it is a pleasure to thank here. Paul Cartledge, Peter Garnsey and David Stone read the complete manuscript and made helpful suggestions. Lorene Sterner prepared the plans and architectural reconstruction. Iveta Adams' meticulous editing removed many errors and inconsistencies. As a sub-field of Classical archaeology the study of ancient households is developing fast and while I have been working on this volume other scholars have also been engaged in addressing similar or related issues to those presented in some of my case studies. I have tried to make reference to as much of this work as possible in my footnotes and 'Bibliographic essay'. My approach in individual Chapters has benefited from exchanging ideas with Bradley Ault, Nicholas Cahill, Alexandra Coucouzeli, Elaine Gazda, Kathleen Lynch, Robin Osborne, Adam Rabinowitz, Monika Trümper, Barbara Tsakirgis and students in graduate and undergraduate seminars on Greek and Roman housing that I have taught at the University of Michigan. I am particularly indebted to Anthony Snodgrass for his staunch and continuing support which has done so much to facilitate my work; his example has inspired in me the courage to tackle major questions and to explore a wide range of evidence, although he is in no way responsible for the result.

Finally, at a practical level, this volume would never have been completed without the kindness of my family who have always supported my education and career, and have helped to create the time and space for me to work. Most recently it has been Dave, and especially Charlotte, who have had to make the greatest sacrifices. I dedicate this book to them all with love and gratitude.

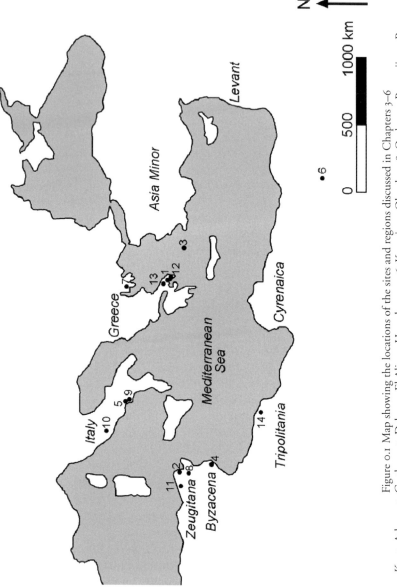

Figure 0.1 Map showing the locations of the sites and regions discussed in Chapters 3–6
Key: 1: Athens; 2: Carthage; 3: Delos; 4: El Alia; 5: Herculaneum; 6: Karanis; 7: Olynthus; 8: Oudna; 9: Pompeii; 10: Rome; 11: Tabarka; 12: Thorikos; 13: Vari; 14: Zliten

Introduction

This volume is about the related concepts of house and household in Classical Antiquity and about how those concepts were materialised at different times and in different places through the physical structure of the house itself. More importantly, it considers how that physical structure and its associated concepts can help to address major questions about social structure, patterns of cultural interaction, continuity and change in Classical Antiquity. The chronological scope is long, ranging from the tenth century BCE (the Early Iron Age) down to the fourth century CE. The geographical spread is equally broad, stretching from modern Turkey in the north east to Tunisia in the south-west, taking in Greece and Italy on the way. My goal, however, is not to present a comprehensive account of everything that is known about housing and households within this span. Instead, the individual chapters constitute case studies based on evidence from specific regions during particular periods. In each instance discussion begins by seeking to understand the appearance, organisation or representation of housing through archaeological, iconographic and/or textual sources, but the aim is much broader. The size, form and decoration of an individual domestic structure are determined by a variety of factors: environment, technology and availability of resources impose broad parameters. Nonetheless, an equally important role is played by culturally specific expectations about the kinds of architecture and decoration that are appropriate, about how and where different activities should be carried out, and by and with whom.

It is those expectations, and the wider social and cultural systems of which they are a part, which this volume seeks to explore. Each chapter pursues one among a variety of possible avenues for the investigation of the questions and evidence presented. While the examination of major issues from a single point of view in this way obviously cannot be comprehensive, my intention is to offer new perspectives on familiar problems, suggesting that a more detailed understanding of one limited aspect can contribute to a clearer picture of the whole. I hope that using the household as a tool in this way will also facilitate more dialogue between the related, but frustratingly separate, areas of academic discourse on the ancient 'family' (based largely on texts) and 'household archaeology' (focused on the material record). At the same time I seek to engage with some of the recent scholarship on domestic space in the Classical world, exploring ways in which it might be possible to push the evidence further in order to address a broader range of issues.

Through the book as a whole I also wish to argue two larger points: first, that while houses, households and families have in recent years become increasingly important as objects of inquiry in Greek and Roman contexts, their potential as sources of information both about domestic life, and about wider social and cultural issues, has yet to be fully realised. Second, and more broadly, in keeping with some recent developments in Classical Studies I wish to support a re-evaluation of the way in which different types of evidence are used, giving greater weight and independence to the material sources in comparison with texts. While the amount of ground this volume covers will undoubtedly mean that it leaves untouched more questions than it is able to address, I hope that it will at least indicate something of the potential of an approach grounded in the material culture as a means of furthering our understanding of the social history of the Greek and Roman worlds. At the same time, I try to evoke some of the fascination of ancient housing as a subject for study and to indicate the power of the household as a lens through which to examine larger social, cultural and historical problems.

CHAPTER I

Domestic space and social organisation

Dwelling is about the active projection of the social and individual
being by means of the artefact.

Humphrey 1988, 18

[F]ocus on the fine-grained relationship between people and the material culture of the home . . . leads to powerful insights into the societies
in question.

Miller 2001, 15

INTRODUCTION

In the 2002 film comedy *My Big Fat Greek Wedding*, the Greek American
screen parents of actress Nia Vardalos host a dinner for her fiancé's White
Anglo-Saxon Protestant mother and father, so that the families can meet
each other for the first time. The event is held at their home in a Chicago
suburb, yet to the guests of honour it is obvious from the outset that this
is not going to be quite the dinner party they had anticipated. Drawing up
at the house they are greeted by a large, extended family gathered outside.
Two whole lambs are roasting on spits over an open fire in the middle of
the front lawn. In the background the house itself is an unremarkable two-
storey building but it has been customised by the owners: an up-and-over
garage door has been painted to resemble a Greek flag, and replica Classical
statues of the Greek goddess Aphrodite watch over the assembled crowds.
As the evening unfolds, the Greek Americans continue to confound their
guests' expectations: a contribution brought to the evening meal has to
be identified as a cake for the hostess. Ushered inside, the visitors find
themselves taking their meal seated on a sofa, where they are offered a
succession of bite-sized morsels, to be washed down with tiny glasses of
spirits.

The film derives its humour from juxtaposing the unconscious assumptions of the two ethnic subgroups. For example, what is meant by

3

'family': from the Greek American point of view, 'meeting the family' includes uncles, aunts and cousins – an extended family group. To their guests, however, the definition is much narrower, limiting itself to the basic nuclear family of husband, wife and any children. The film encourages us to question some of our expectations about a variety of activities that we would not normally stop to think about: what kind of an occasion do we envisage when invited to someone's house for dinner? Where do we normally cook a meal? What food do we eat, and where and how do we serve it? There are in fact many ways these simple actions could be performed, yet from early childhood we become accustomed to certain patterns of behaviour. If we choose to adopt them, then we implicitly define ourselves as belonging to a particular community and we accept our allotted place within it. (So, Vardalos' character dutifully helps her mother to prepare for the evening's festivities beforehand by helping her to chop vegetables, but when her brother enters the kitchen it is his role to sit and eat as much food as possible.)

Vardalos' story may be fiction, but the underlying premise is one her audience will recognise: unconscious patterns of domestic activity can be just as revealing about someone's cultural background and sense of identity as overt symbols like the Greek flag and the replicas of Aphrodite. The same principle has motivated academic studies by anthropologists, sociologists and scholars in a range of other related disciplines who have investigated numerous cultures throughout the world. Their findings show that there are a wide variety of ways in which households can potentially function as units to meet the basic needs of individual members for food, shelter and social contact. In any one society the manner in which domestic activities are organised and the roles individuals play are determined by cultural factors. These include the status accorded to different social groups (women, men, the elderly, children, servants and so on) and beliefs about how those groups should interact. Thus the daily performance of routine household tasks maps out relationships, establishing and reinforcing social structures and norms. Bringing up children to assume their correct place in a household is a means of passing on cultural values to the next generation. Study of the organisation of activities within households therefore provides an important resource for understanding how societies define and perpetuate themselves and how they change through time and space. Such research has important implications for understanding past societies, including those of the Greek and Roman worlds, showing that the household is an essential topic for study in its own right. Perhaps even more importantly, such work also demonstrates that households offer a window through which to view many aspects of society as a whole: because what goes on inside a household is inseparable from its broader social and cultural context, households offer a means of addressing questions about, for example, the relative status assigned to men and women, or the amount of differentiation between rich and poor, citizen and non-citizen, or indigenous groups and settlers. Households can therefore reveal not only wider social systems but also the effects of larger-scale political, economic and social change.

Research on Greek and Roman households has tended to concentrate on their organisation, functioning and internal social dynamics. Archaeological study has focused largely on the physical layout and decoration of excavated houses. Where an attempt has been made to view the domestic environment as a lived space as well as an architectural structure, the main emphasis has been on understanding how the arrangement of rooms, artefacts and decoration may have been designed to support particular kinds of social relationships. For example, prompted by the view of housing expressed in surviving texts, the elite houses of Roman Italy have been interpreted as having been designed to enhance the wealth and status of their male owners through elaborate decoration (see Chapter 5), while in relation to Classical Greece, debate has centred on the extent to which women were segregated from men in domestic contexts. It is normally impossible to use the excavated evidence to follow the histories of individual households and their members through time. Instead the volume of evidence, the variety of dates and locations from which it comes, and the range of social groups represented, all enable us to look at more general cultural patterns. For example, we can assess what factors were important in structuring households, evaluate what may have been typical behaviour and what may have been exceptional, pay attention to social groups whose voices are rarely heard through the surviving texts, and look for continuities and discontinuities between different periods and areas.

Alongside archaeological study a second area of research has involved using texts and inscriptions to examine social relationships between individual family members. This has shed light on a wide range of topics, from the degree of affection between husband and wife or parents and their children, to inheritance and the passing of property rights between generations. While providing numerous insights into family life, such studies have rarely intersected with investigations of the archaeological evidence. One reason is that although 'household' (a group of people living together under the same roof) and 'family' (a group of people related to each other by blood or by marriage) are sometimes used interchangeably, they are not the same thing. Identifying the social groups living in the houses found on Greek and Roman sites during excavation is notoriously difficult. Nuclear families may have dominated in some periods and locations, while extended ones may have been more common in others. Patterns of residence may also have varied according to a household's social and economic status. In addition, each individual household would have had its own 'life cycle': as today, its composition is likely to have changed through time as children were born, grew up and moved away, while elderly relatives may have moved in, and spouses may have died or been divorced and new marriages taken place. Evidence of all of these processes taking place in Graeco-Roman Antiquity can be found in surviving written sources, but they are difficult or impossible to trace through the material record.

My aim in this volume is to build on previous work in both of these areas in a number of ways. By exploring how analytical methods might be refined and how previous conclusions might be extended to include new data, I attempt to suggest more nuanced views of households in familiar contexts. At the same time I also try to broaden the scope of discussion to include topics lying beyond the boundaries of the house itself, asking what the study of households can lead us to conclude about larger social and cultural issues where text-based study has had much to say. The individual chapters that follow deal with a selection of chronological periods and geographical locations, and each one aims primarily to address a different issue. There are, however, a number of themes which naturally recur. Perhaps one of the most fundamental is the extent to which a distinction between the 'public' and 'private' spheres is applicable to discussions of the ancient world. In modern western society this opposition underpins our definitions of house and home, and the terms have often been used by scholars in relation to both Greek and Roman housing (for example Leach 2004). Nevertheless, ethnographic study has demonstrated that concepts such as privacy are not universal, they are specific to contemporary western culture and cannot be applied in other cultural contexts (Kent 1991, 32 n. 1). In fact the terms as they are understood in the West today took on their present meaning only relatively recently. As ancient historians have suggested, redefining the domestic and public spheres to make them applicable to Greek and Roman societies is not a straightforward task; rather than being static, their definitions may have been contested and subject to shifts through time. It seems, therefore, that specific locations and periods demand either their own tailored definitions of the private sphere, or even the total replacement of this concept by other ways of defining the sets of activities appropriate to different physical settings.

One means of approaching this issue is by looking at representations of domestic activities in literary and artistic sources. These are revealing, not so much as depictions of the appearance and use of actual structures or architectural spaces, but as windows into the conceptual world surrounding the household, an approach explored in detail in Chapter 6 in relation to the symbolic value of representations of villa architecture in urban houses of Roman North Africa. But the archaeological evidence for the house itself provides a starting point for the consideration of these issues, offering an insight into the degree of flexibility in the conceptual boundaries between different spheres which in turn can indicate underlying social conventions such as the amount of interaction expected between members of the household and outsiders. Examination of the domestic context as a single system can reveal something of the range of activities considered to be appropriate to it in different places and at different times.

Even cursory study shows that residential buildings often acted as the backdrop for a number of activities that would not necessarily take place in a private home today, so that defining a 'house' is not always as straightforward as one might assume. While some of the functions central to domestic life are familiar, such as storing, preparing and consuming food, there are others which we would not necessarily think of as 'domestic' in character. A household may often have produced many of the items needed for daily life with, for instance, spinning and weaving textiles commonly taking place in the home in both Greek and Roman contexts. Urban houses, as well as farms, could be used for storing sufficient crops produced on the household's own land. Those crops could also be processed in the house itself to make flour, olive oil and wine. In addition, small-scale workshops were sometimes integrated into domestic buildings and manufactured a wide range of items including pottery, sculpture and metalwork. Some of the processes involved must have created levels of noise, heat and smell which might be considered unacceptable in a residential neighbourhood in a modern western city, again emphasising the differences in expectations between different cultures. Retail shops were also a feature of houses in many settlements throughout Antiquity. There is thus a blurring of the boundaries we might expect to see in western contexts today between domestic, industrial and commercial activities, as well as between what we might consider the private and the public spheres.

A further fundamental issue which underlies much of this volume has already been touched on in the opening to this chapter, and that is the role played by houses in articulating the identities of both the household as a group, and various of its members individually. This is one of the most complex aspects of the domestic sphere, but it has a great deal to offer as a means of addressing a range of social questions and therefore receives considerable emphasis here. Expressions of identity in the domestic context are potentially very variable: they may be both conscious and unconscious and may involve assertions about membership of social, cultural and ethnic groups as well as about social, economic or even political status. A single house can simultaneously convey a number of messages about different aspects of identity, or indeed about a variety of identities. This can be done through a range of elements including architecture and decoration, as well as the organisation of rooms and exterior spaces, their relationship to each other, and the uses to which they are put. Messages may sometimes be mixed, or even contradictory, with, for example, contrasting cultural affiliations expressed by the architecture of a house and by the pattern of use of the internal rooms.

By viewing each individual house as part of a wider group and comparing aspects of the domestic environment across that group, such tensions can be explored and their underlying causes unraveled. This method can also be used to investigate whether patterns of elite culture are espoused by households lower down the socio-economic scale, or whether members of different social and economic groups have their own distinctive sets of values and subcultures. A similar strategy can also be used to study patterns of interaction between contemporaneous societies: for example, there has recently been a great deal of important and far-reaching debate over the expansion of the Roman world and its consequences both for the Mediterranean cultures with which Rome came into contact, and for Rome itself. Study of individual households on Delos (Chapter 4), where Greek, Italian and Near Eastern inhabitants shared the same settlement space, enables the applicability and explanatory power of different models for cultural change to be explored in one specific and well-defined context.

The example of Delos highlights another major theme of the volume as a whole, and that is the comparison of Greek with Roman domestic culture. Early approaches placed Greek and Roman housing into a single evolutionary continuum in which Roman domestic architecture was viewed (like many other aspects of Roman culture) as deriving ultimately from Greek models. Through time, however, an increase in the available archaeological evidence, particularly from Greek sites, has made contrasts between structures of different dates and from different parts of the ancient world increasingly apparent. Questions and interpretative models have simultaneously become more sophisticated. Recent studies have attempted to unravel the extent to which Greek architectural forms, such as the colonnaded peristyle courtyard, influenced the creation of Roman ones. But there are also broader questions to be asked about the relationship between the two cultures in connection with their construction and conceptualisation of the domestic sphere: do similar architectural forms indicate comparable ways of using the house, for example as a tool in social relationships? Did both Greek and Roman households manipulate their domestic architecture as a means of articulating status and identity to the same degree and in comparable ways? And does a comparison between the two cultures of the way in which the domestic sphere responded to broader social, cultural and political change help to improve our understanding of the processes involved? Placing detailed studies of different aspects of the domestic sphere in Greek and Roman contexts side by side in this volume is not meant to imply a return to the single evolutionary framework invoked by early archaeological research on ancient housing. But it is intended to provide an opportunity to make implicit comparisons of this kind, enabling conclusions to be drawn about the relationship between the two cultures and about some of the general processes that can be seen to operate either in one or in both of them.

I return to some of these issues in the Epilogue to this volume. For the moment, however, it is necessary to lay the groundwork for addressing these larger questions by defining the object of inquiry more closely. The remainder of this chapter considers, first, what the excavated evidence tells us in general terms about ancient houses as physical spaces and the sorts of constraints they imposed on social practice; and second, what kind of conceptual framework we can use to try to understand and interpret the physical evidence. This sets the scene for more detailed discussion of the individual cultural contexts and their associated data sets presented in each of the succeeding case studies.

ANCIENT HOUSES AS PHYSICAL PLACES

To a casual visitor at an excavated Greek or Roman town today the residential areas are often the most difficult to visualise as inhabited spaces. In Greek contexts in particular, the materials used in construction tended to be less durable than those employed in public architecture: unlike temples and theatres, which are often built entirely in stone, house walls were often founded on stone socles (bases) but the superstructure was generally made of mud-brick (blocks of sun-dried, unfired mud). This was the traditional construction method used in many parts of Greece until the twentieth century and it has obvious advantages: the raw materials – mud with added sand, silt and vegetable-matter – are normally readily available at or close to the building site, and mud-brick offers good insulation against summer daytime heat and winter cold. As ethnographic studies in modern contexts have shown, making the bricks is also a quick process and can be done without extensive specialist knowledge, so that with the help of friends and neighbours families can construct their own homes (Sutton 1999, 84). An obvious difficulty, however, is that mud-brick is very vulnerable to erosion by moisture, which effectively dissolves the individual blocks. For this reason walls built in this way require careful construction and maintenance. A coating of lime plaster on the exterior protects the surface, while the use of a stone socle reduces the chances of rain pooling against the bases of the exterior walls and undermining them, and it also increases load-bearing capacity enabling the construction of upper storeys. A pitched roof of thatch or terracotta tile with deeply overhanging eaves also helps to prevent rain water reaching the outside walls.

The long-lived and widespread use of mud-brick buildings, not only in the Mediterranean but also in hot, dry climates in other parts of the world such as the American south-west, shows how effective they are. But once the inhabitants cease to renew the protective plaster coating on the exterior and to maintain the roof in watertight condition, decay rapidly sets in. Roofs and upper floors would originally have been supported on timber joists, but except in arid desert environments such as Egypt, wood does not survive once exposed to the elements, and its decay causes further collapse. Where terracotta tiles were used on the roof, provided they were not salvaged when the building was abandoned, they are generally preserved in archaeological deposits as a thick layer, sealing the remains of the house. Underneath, the fallen mud-bricks have normally dissolved and become soil deposits overlying the house floors. Once these are removed, what remains is the low stone socle, often only two or three courses high, which reveals the layout of the house's ground floor and says something about the character of some of the rooms. In the earliest Greek houses the floors themselves were compacted earth. By the Classical period additional materials were sometimes used, especially on exterior surfaces that were exposed to rain: these could be composed of mortar or paved or cobbled.

A more decorative effect was achieved with mosaics. At around 400 BCE when these were first introduced, they were composed of black and white or coloured pebbles laid in patterns into a mortar matrix. From the fourth century onwards specially cut tesserae or cubes of stone or terracotta were laid in designs which became increasingly complex into the Hellenistic period. By the Roman era the repertoire of designs could include representations of the natural world and human activities, as well as geometric patterns. At this time a further decorative flooring technique was introduced, opus sectile, which was composed of stone pieces cut into different shapes and again forming complex, usually geometrical, patterns. Other decorative elements were also gradually introduced over time, and grew more elaborate and widespread during the Roman period. These include the use of stone to create decorative architectural elements such as columns and window mullions (from the Classical period onwards). Painted wall plaster, initially used to create plain panels, also came to include elaborate designs showing, for example, representations of architectural fantasies and human and divine figures.

Surviving evidence of architectural features like these gives a general impression of how a house was laid out on the ground floor and of some of the main amenities it provided. Except in rare cases such as Delos (Chapter 4) or Pompeii (Chapter 5), it is more difficult to reconstruct the superstructure, to detect the presence of any upstairs rooms, and to find out more about how the different spaces may have been used by their occupants. For information on these questions it is necessary to look in more detail at the finds, the objects mixed in with the soil overlying the house floors. Many of the original furnishings used in Greek houses have long since decayed at most sites. A glimpse of what has been lost is provided by the Graeco-Roman town of Karanis, in the Fayum region of Egypt. Because of the dry, desert environment, materials which are normally destroyed by moisture were well preserved. In the residential parts of the settlement excavators found mud-brick walls, some still standing to a height of several storeys underneath the accumulated desert sand (Plate 1.1). Construction elements such as wooden doors and shutters were still in place. Lying in the individual rooms were a wealth of objects including personal items such as wooden combs and children's toys. A variety of equipment was also found such as wooden agricultural and kitchen implements, and woven palm-leaf baskets (Plate 1.2). Alongside these were fabrics used for furnishing and clothing.

The extraordinary level of preservation at Karanis gives an idea of the kinds of items whose presence can be detected only indirectly in houses from other parts of the Greek and Roman worlds. The relatively late date of the site, which was occupied from the third century BCE to the fifth century CE, also contributes to the richness of the collection of artefacts found in the houses, since there seems to have been a tendency for the number and variety of domestic objects in the ancient world generally to increase through time. Nevertheless, much can still be learned, even

Plate 1.1 View east over House c65 at the Graeco-Roman town of Karanis (Egypt), showing the mud-brick architecture preserved due to the dry conditions. Photographed during the University of Michigan excavations of 1928–1935

from houses at earlier, less well preserved sites, by collecting as detailed information as possible about the objects which do survive. Of the various types of finds, ceramic items are normally the most numerous throughout the period discussed in this volume. The majority were originally used for the transportation, storage, preparation and serving of food and drink, although pottery was used for other purposes as well, for example to make containers for perfume and cosmetics. It is frequently fragments that are found rather than whole objects or vessels.

In certain soil conditions the use of specialised recovery techniques can reveal evidence of some of the contents of containers through chemical analysis of their interior surfaces. Further, shells and discarded bones from meat, poultry and even fish sometimes survive on floors and in rubbish deposits in good enough condition for their species to be identified. Around fireplaces or where a house has been burned down, traces of plant foods are also sometimes preserved by charring, and can include various kinds of grain such as wheat and barley, and legumes such as lentils. In addition to food containers, other objects were also made of pottery including weights

Plate 1.2 A woven palm-leaf basket recovered during the University of Michigan Karanis excavations (Kelsey Museum accession number 0000.00.8528)

used on looms for producing cloth, oil lamps (from the Archaic period onwards), and decorative architectural elements such as relief plaques (from the Classical period onwards). Terracotta (fired clay) was also used in water systems: although piped water came into homes relatively late (not until the Hellenistic or Roman periods), terracotta pipes were used to supply public fountain houses from the Archaic period and are found in domestic contexts for drainage. Terracotta chamber pots and hip baths are also found from the Classical period onwards although these were not plumbed in: water had to be carried from elsewhere and the vessels had to be emptied by hand.

More infrequent types of finds include metal items. Some of these are small components of larger items which have not survived: for instance the original presence of wooden doors, shutters and pieces of furniture is sometimes revealed by bronze or iron nails, bosses, hinges and locks. Implements for subsistence activities are also sometimes represented by their constituent parts, such as iron blades or bronze fish-hooks. Other large items such as cups and serving vessels were sometimes made of bronze, silver, or even gold, but these are seldom found in domestic contexts because they must have been expensive and are therefore likely to have been removed before or during the abandonment or destruction of a house. Smaller metal articles are sometimes found, though: in addition to coins, which were introduced in the Archaic period, these include bronze probes and items of dress such as pins and jewellery. Bone and ivory were sometimes also used for items such as pins and these occasionally also survive. Finally, the most substantial types of finds are large stone objects which range from the decorative to the functional. Among the former are components for pieces of furniture such as Classical Greek wash basins (louteria) and Roman tables (cartibula). More functional items include hand querns (found from the Early Iron Age onwards) and large mills (in Roman contexts), both used for grinding grain into flour. From the Classical period onwards press beds and counterweight blocks from large olive- and wine-presses are also found.

Items such as these can be very important indicators of a range of activities. Used in combination with architectural information the spatial distribution of the objects can also be significant, suggesting where particular activities were carried out and also, more indirectly, which members of the household may have used different particular areas if individual types of items can be connected with specific users. Such conclusions have to be drawn with caution: as well as turning up in the places in which they were used, objects may also be found where they were stored, or even discarded. There are also a number of factors which could have caused them to be moved from where they were originally deposited, including the circumstances under which the house was abandoned, subsequent human activity on the site (for example, further building), natural processes such as erosion, and the actions of the excavators themselves. The combination of all these factors (known as site formation processes) means that, while it is important to study the distribution of movable objects, that distribution is not always easy to interpret (see Chapter 5).

Artefacts also change through time in various ways and to varying degrees. These changes encompass the materials and technology used to manufacture them, and the styles and forms they take. Systematic cataloguing of such changes is one of the techniques which enable individual structures to be dated by archaeologists. Some of the most detailed information comes from pottery, both because it is such a common material and because styles and forms often seem to have changed relatively rapidly, so that in some of the periods covered by this book ceramicists conventionally date vessels to within a twenty-five or thirty-year span. These dates are established in a variety of ways. At the city of Olynthus, for example, pottery and other artefacts were recovered from an archaeological deposit which seemingly results from an historical event – the sack of the city by Philip II of Macedon in 348 BCE – which we know about from documentary sources and which is assumed to have caused the abandonment of the city. If this assumption is correct, then all of the finds in the houses can be said to have been manufactured in or before 348 BCE. Where similar items are recovered from domestic interiors at other sites for which we do not have any historical evidence, they can offer an approximate year before which a building must have been constructed. If they are found beneath its foundations, however, they offer a date after which the house must have been built. This kind of dating can be done with different levels of precision in different contexts, depending on the numbers of artefacts found, the extent to which items remained undisturbed by later activity and how well the styles of artefact used in different places and at different times are known.[1]

Alterations in the form, style and technology of the buildings themselves and the architectural features they contain can be used alongside the finds for dating purposes. Through time there is a gradual rise in the number and variety of the furnishings and small items included in domestic contexts which is paralleled by a dramatic increase in the size of the largest domestic buildings and by changes in the technology available to construct them. The residential quarters of Roman towns tend to be much more evocative than those of Greek ones since their houses often survive better. Mud-brick is frequently replaced by more durable materials such as stone, and concrete, fired brick and window glass were introduced. These innovations were accompanied by a growth in the size and density of the largest settlements and by an increase in the construction of multiple dwellings, structures housing a number of different households under one roof and equivalent in function to today's blocks of flats or apartments, if not necessarily similar in design. (Such structures are also attested for Classical Greece in literary sources but are difficult to identify archaeologically.) By Imperial times, the largest houses bear little structural resemblance to the houses of the Greek Early Iron Age. The contrasts between these domestic environments result not only from advances in technology but also from social, economic and political changes. It is these underlying developments, and some of the

---

[1] For the houses included in this volume I have generally followed the published dates assigned by the excavators, who have the best overview of their material. Where sites are being compared I have tried to minimise inconsistencies caused by differences in the availability of precise pottery chronologies and in methods of assigning dates, by trying to standardise dates to rough periods – as will be evident from some of the graphs in Chapters 2 and 3.

ways in which they can be studied through the archaeological evidence of housing, which are the central theme of this book. But before they can be addressed, it is important to think about how this can be done using the kind of information about the physical remains of housing just outlined.

The situation represented in the film *My Big Fat Greek Wedding* and discussed at the opening of this chapter is useful in highlighting the extent to which patterns of domestic activity are culturally determined. It also demonstrates just how difficult it is to set aside our own upbringing and perspective, even simply to understand the behaviour of other inhabitants of our own communities. While the situation is fictitious, the problem is a real one. The challenge – and the necessity – of being aware of and suppressing our unconscious assumptions is, of course, much greater when we come to study the societies of other areas and other periods. Interpreting the kinds of empty and partially preserved spaces surviving from Greek and Roman Antiquity is no easy task, and the very fact that there is unquestionably a close connection between a household's broader cultural context and the minutiae of its daily activities means that many of the aspects of domestic life we take for granted today must have been very different in the past. We should therefore try to avoid projecting our own conceptual frameworks back into Classical Antiquity. Two strategies are useful here and can function in combination: first, being conscious of the relationship between different patterns of domestic spatial behaviour and wider social systems in other cultures can help us to set aside our own cultural prejudices and to build up what anthropologists refer to as an 'etic' perspective, a way of taking an abstracted, external view of the material. Second, studying the surviving textual evidence can take us a step further, helping to reconstruct some of the ways in which the ancients themselves might have viewed and interpreted their own domestic environments, building towards an 'emic' perspective.

Cross-cultural comparisons highlight the fact that the social groups living together under one roof can vary enormously in their composition. There is little evidence from Antiquity for the single-person domestic unit which has become increasingly common in modern western society, but the basic nuclear and extended family groups mentioned above are just two among a constellation of possible types of social unit. These can also comprise much more diverse groupings, many of which have their own distinctive house-forms. Among them are the 'houseful' (which includes unrelated individuals such as friends, lodgers, servants or slaves); households occupying a cluster of separate buildings within a perimeter wall; and even whole village communities living together in a single 'long-house'. While these forms of household may not at first sight seem very relevant to the Greek and Roman worlds, recent research has raised the possibility that each one may in fact have been present in a particular time and location in Classical Antiquity – a reminder that ancient society was more diverse than we might think, and that it is important to explore that diversity before using household structure as a basis for discussing wider social, political and economic issues.[2]

Research carried out in a variety of disciplines including architecture, sociology, ethnoarchaeology and prehistoric archaeology provides a variety of models for domestic behaviour and for ways in which different behavioural patterns are mapped out spatially within the house, showing that architectural features and activity areas respond to the particular requirements of individual social patterns and structures. Such studies of other cultures enable us to see connections between specific spatial configurations, modes of behaviour and their associated ideologies. We cannot, of course, assume that there is a one-to-one correspondence. Nor should we think that any of these comparative examples is necessarily a close match for any ancient society. Nonetheless, such information is valuable in suggesting dimensions of the material record which might be revealing about particular aspects of social behaviour and ideology. At the same time these studies can alert us to some of the unthinking assumptions we might make about the use of domestic space based on our own cultural experiences and show us something of the much wider range of ways in which that space might be used, opening our eyes to new possibilities for interpreting the ancient evidence. Indeed, a striking aspect of this comparative material is the great variation in the way domestic interiors are structured. In many cases the inside is subdivided to a limited degree or not at all. This does not mean, however, that there is a lack of order in the way space is used. As many examples of single-room dwellings show, specific domestic tasks often still have customary locations ('activity areas'), even if those locations are not defined by walls. The same can also apply to the movements of individuals, which again can be limited to certain parts of a single-room house even if there are no physical barriers demarcating separate spaces for them. (Patterns of behaviour associated with single-room dwellings are

---

[2] For example, housefuls have been suggested for Imperial Rome (Wallace-Hadrill 2003), house compounds for Early Iron Age Greece (Mazarakis Ainian 2007), and long-house communities for Early Iron Age Greece (Coucouzeli 1998).

discussed further in connection with the houses of Early Iron Age Greece in Chapter 2.)

Where domestic interiors are subdivided into multiple spaces (some of which may be unroofed), it becomes clear that the concepts by which those spaces are categorised are also often very unfamiliar: for example, the modern western provision of separate areas for particular social and biological activities (eating, sleeping, washing, relaxing in company and so on) is frequently unknown in more traditional societies. Similarly, the allocation of special rooms for individual household members (bedrooms, nurseries, home offices and so on) is particularly associated with modern western society, which carries a relatively high valuation of the individual as opposed to the group (Pader 1997, 71). Other ways of organising space involve the use of alternative social categories. Whole groups may habitually use a single space: for example, in some societies of the modern Arab world complex rules govern the behaviour of women, in particular restricting social interaction with unrelated men. Study of housing from such societies reveals some of the architectural techniques which help to support these social rules. Identification of similar devices in Classical Greek houses suggests the operation of similar kinds of social restrictions, albeit they are underpinned by a very different ideological framework (Nevett 1994).

This variety in patterns of behaviour highlights the need to study ancient housing without unconsciously making assumptions about the use of domestic space based on our own cultural experiences. Even though it is a common practice (for example Leach 2004, esp. 18–54), using familiar words to describe the spaces in ancient houses ('kitchen', for instance) can have the unintended consequence of conjuring up a whole range of very specific patterns of use associated with those rooms in our own culture – patterns which may be very different from the way in which spaces were used in ancient houses, even if some of the activities were the same. For example, in modern western society we might visualise a kitchen as a place where, in addition to food being prepared, food and utensils might be stored and informal dining might take place. Thus, if finds of utensils for preparing food in an ancient house are interpreted as evidence of a 'kitchen', we might be tempted to assume a similar range of other activities took place here. In reality, however, storage of food and/or dining may customarily have taken place elsewhere in Greek or Roman houses. For this reason it is preferable (if more long-winded) to use more neutral terms such as 'food preparation area'.

Specific insights suggested by particular ethnographic examples are brought into the discussion of the different data sets in following chapters as they become relevant. But having highlighted some alternative ways of conceptualising and viewing space, I want to turn now to how study and comparison of surviving ancient textual sources enable us to begin to reconstruct ancient ways of thinking about and using the domestic environment, replacing some of the assumptions based on our own experience of domestic space with ideas coming directly from the ancient world. Although Greek and Roman authors include only relatively few detailed descriptions of houses and how they were used, there are a number of briefer, incidental references to particular rooms or events taking place in people's homes from different periods and contexts. Like most of our literary evidence from the ancient world, these are generally written by members of the elite, and offer only the limited perspective of the male householder or male visitor, but they do provide an insight into some of the underlying cultural attitudes towards the use of space, and taken together they are an important resource. Many of the conclusions they suggest are specific to particular periods, locations and/or types of house, and these are discussed at relevant points in later chapters. But a few more general observations also emerge which serve to illustrate some of the differences between the ancient and the modern experience of dwelling.

Perhaps the most striking point is the strong influence of the external environment on the organisation of activities inside the house. In the absence of the technology we have today to modify our surroundings, such as heating, air conditioning and electric lighting, housing had to be designed in order to withstand climatic extremes and make use of natural light. A variety of Greek and Roman writers comment that the main living apartments of a house faced south to benefit from the warming effects of the low, angled rays of the winter sunshine which warmed the interior, and this corresponds to what is found archaeologically. These authors also indicate that there was a great deal of flexibility in how space was used, and this must partly also be explained by climatic factors: while a large room with a central hearth would have been warm and cheerful on cold winter days, in the heat of summer an exterior location would have made a cooler and better-ventilated, more comfortable working environment for domestic chores. Archaeological evidence suggests that both types of place were often used for such activities, and exterior spaces seem to have been of great importance, not only as extensions of the interior rooms which could be used for domestic chores, but also as a means of admitting light and air into the interiors of houses of all sizes.

The ancient authors, particularly those writing in Latin, also suggest that there was a complex layering of different social roles within the house.

As well as the issue of gender mentioned above, other relevant dimensions of social identity include status (such as free or slave), membership of the household (resident or visitor) and age (child, adult or elderly). These categories cross-cut each other in such a way that a single individual falls into several groups simultaneously. The extent to which each category is important in a particular culture varies depending on the time period, geographical location and social and economic status of the households under examination. In order for a specific aspect of social identity to be suited to investigation through the domestic sphere, the house needs to have been an important location for affirming or contesting it in the context in question. For example, gender relations and a need to distinguish between household members and visitors seem to have been major influences on the organisation of domestic space in Classical Greece (Chapter 3), but less so in Early Imperial Italy, where the wealth and status of the male householder and his need to use the house as a tool in social and political relationships with his peers and inferiors seems to carry greater weight (Chapter 5).

While textual evidence provides a useful guide to the cultural context for some of the archaeology, and in some cases offers a framework for trying to interpret the material record, there are also some potential pitfalls in trying to bring the two types of source together. Perhaps most misleading is the problem of identifying particular rooms, or indeed items of furnishing, mentioned in the texts. Excavators of sites where housing has been found have routinely adopted terms used by ancient authors as labels for spaces they have uncovered. But while the identification of spaces such as the atrium and peristyle, which have characteristic architectural features, is likely to correspond broadly with the kinds of spaces the texts refer to, the situation is more problematic in relation to rooms which have fewer such features or which are mentioned rarely and in passing without much discussion or description. This difficulty means that Vitruvius, and other ancient authors, need to be read critically and with an awareness that we cannot always be certain that we can identify the rooms they are talking about. For this reason when trying to understand the way in which space was used in excavated structures it is often preferable to avoid using most Greek or Latin terms.

At the start of this chapter I pointed out that we intuitively tend to interpret choices made in the organisation, decoration and use of contemporary living spaces as indicators about a range of aspects of the occupants' identities and their social and cultural lives. As we have seen in the last two sections, while this basic principle offers the possibility that excavated housing can provide insights into the ancient world, interpreting the evidence is far from straightforward. Many of the clues we use in such situations in our everyday lives are lacking in archaeological contexts since only a limited range of the furnishings, and sometimes only relatively little of the architecture, normally survive. An even more challenging barrier to interpretation is the gulf which exists between our own world and that of the ancient Greeks and Romans. While it might be tempting to assume that many of the underlying principles by which their houses were organised were similar to our own, this is obviously dangerous. Ethnographic study shows how variable the organisation and use of domestic space can be and also highlights the complexity of the relationship between the different aspects of social life played out in domestic contexts. At the same time, the more closely and critically ancient texts are examined, the more they reveal differences between the way in which domestic space was conceptualised in antiquity, and the way in which it is thought about and used in modern western society. As I suggest in the chapters which follow, rather than being a hindrance, this complexity and these cultural differences offer the opportunity to use ancient housing as a means of deepening our understanding of Greek and Roman culture and how each society varied through space and time.

CHAPTER 2

House-form and social complexity: the transformation of Early Iron Age Greece

Bronze walls led in all directions from the doorway to the inside and the cornice around them was blue; gold doors opened into the carefully built house; silver doorposts stood over the bronze threshold, with a silver lintel above and a gold handle; on each side there were gold and silver dogs... Inside there were seats all along the walls from the doorway to the interior and on them were fine, well-made fabrics, women's handiwork... And gold boys stood on well-made bases holding bright torches in their hands, shining at night for diners in the house.

Homer, *Odyssey* 7.86–97

The organization of the built environment and use of space is a metaphor for the organization of a culture; the former are the visible, tangible expressions of invisible, intangible culture. The amount of segmentation present in a culture structures its architecture and spatial patterns...

Kent 1991, 31

INTRODUCTION: ISSUES AND APPROACHES

Homeric descriptions like that of the extensive and opulent palace of King Alcinoös in the *Odyssey*, quoted above represent our earliest surviving descriptions of housing from the ancient Greek world. Nineteenth- and early twentieth-century archaeologists were tempted to associate these poetically imagined structures with the monumental palatial buildings being unearthed at the time at sites such as Tiryns and Mycenae. But it became clear that whereas the palaces were probably destroyed before 1200 BCE, the Homeric poems did not come together in their final form until about the eighth century BCE. Archaeological remains of housing dating to the eighth century itself suggest that at this time the Greek population was actually resident in small, relatively plain and undifferentiated houses rather than in the kinds of magnificent structures described in the poems. At the same

22

time, however, the Homeric texts show that there was some awareness in the collective imagination that residential structures could potentially be manipulated in order to convey messages about the prosperity and status of their occupants, through elements such as scale and decoration. This chapter uses archaeological evidence to trace the way in which the idea of a large and well-furnished house began to become a reality in Greek communities during the Early Iron Age, from about 1000 BCE to 500 BCE, exploring the social significance of changes in the layout of houses during that period.

Much research has been devoted to the Greek Early Iron Age because it was a time of profound transformation: out of a series of relatively small, village-type communities emerged a network of complex citizen-states (or poleis) including Classical Athens. It has become clear that a wide range of different aspects of life were involved in these changes, including farming practices, levels of population, the nature of relationships between elite and non-elite social groups, and trading links within and beyond the Greek world. Nevertheless, scholars investigating this revolution have yet to reach a consensus about its speed, timing and causal mechanisms. The reconfiguration of the domestic environment is just one element in this much larger picture. Each household (or *oikos*) must both have participated in and been affected by these developments, so that investigating houses offers an important means of studying this transformation.

In contrast with the other chapters in this volume, for much of the period covered in this chapter it is difficult to use contemporary written accounts as an aid to interpreting the archaeological remains. The Homeric poems have been shown to be of limited relevance as sources of information about any aspect of Greek society at any single place and time (Morris 1997, 558–559) and, as we have already seen, they contain ideas which are not always representative of a single contemporary reality. Other texts offer only limited and fragmentary evidence which rarely has a direct bearing on the character and functioning of individual households. Archaeological remains of the structures themselves are therefore a fundamental source for understanding even the most basic patterns of domestic social relationships. The buildings in question are generally relatively unimpressive and poorly preserved, stone footings for the walls revealing the original plan but with little remaining of the original superstructure. Discussion has often been dominated by detailed examination of evidence from a small number of sites. Nevertheless, it is actually possible to assemble a sample of more than 130 more or less completely excavated houses from Greece and the culturally Greek settlements on the west coast of Asia Minor together, dating between the tenth and sixth centuries BCE. The volume of this evidence makes it possible to adopt a quantitative approach which enables individual sites and structures to be understood as part of a wider picture. Not only does this reveal whether individual houses and groups of houses are likely to be typical or exceptional, but, also, it sheds some light on regionalism and on change through time.

The distribution of the excavated houses through time and space is rather uneven. They date primarily to the eighth and seventh centuries BCE, which is the period when some of the most extensively investigated sites were occupied. Numbers from the tenth and ninth centuries BCE are tiny, and evidence from the sixth century is also limited. The geographical distribution is similarly uneven, with most of the houses located at a relatively small number of sites. This clustering makes it impossible to group the different structures into small regional categories like those which have often been used to analyse pottery, metalwork and other forms of material culture dating to the earlier part of this period (for example Coldstream 1977, Snodgrass 2001). Nevertheless, it is possible to distinguish between houses in four larger areas which have been argued to represent different 'cultural zones' between the late eighth and early fifth centuries BCE (Morris 1998). The majority of known structures lie in the central Greek zone, with lower totals in the western and eastern zones and only very small numbers in the northern zone (see Figure 2.1). These patterns of distribution through time and space are important for two reasons: first, they influence the questions which can be asked and the way in which the material can be analysed. Second, they raise questions about the distribution of the ancient population and how that may have changed through time. Both of these issues are taken into account below in interpreting the material.

THE NATURE OF THE EVIDENCE

Buildings of this period are frequently relatively ephemeral and poorly preserved so that interpretation has tended to focus on the ground plans, with similarities and differences being used to establish a typological framework. In particular, a fundamental distinction is customarily drawn between structures which are apsidal (with at least one curvilinear wall) or oval on the one hand, and those which are orthogonal (in which all the walls are straight) on the other. This contrast in form seems to have been influenced to some extent by the available building materials: the orthogonal buildings are generally stone, sometimes with a mud-brick superstructure, and they probably had flat mud roofs. The curvilinear structures generally had

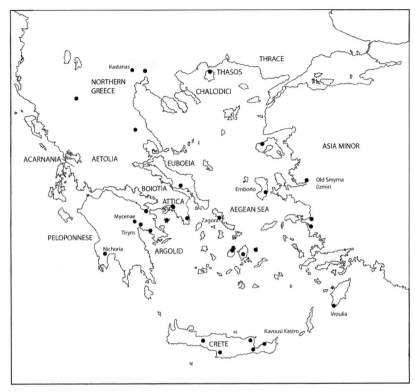

Figure 2.1 Map showing the geographical distribution of the sites analysed in this chapter
and the locations of those discussed in the text. The four regions are as follows:
Central Greece: Attica, the Argolid, southern Euboea, the southern Aegean islands, the
southern Chalkidiki, coastal Thrace, coastal Asia Minor from Old Smyrna
southwards.
Northern Greece: includes the northern mainland together with the northern
Chalkidiki and inland Thrace.
Western Greece: the Peloponnese, mainland Greece from Boiotia to Acarnania and
Aetolia.
Crete: the island of Crete.

stone foundations with a mud-brick or a wattle and daub superstructure
and a pitched thatched roof, making more use of large timbers. It has
sometimes been observed that orthogonal structures are the rule in Crete
and the Greek islands, where suitable building stone was readily available, but that curvilinear buildings were more common in the central and
northern Greek mainland, which had better access to timber. As noted in
Chapter 1, grouping curvilinear buildings together using shared party walls

is difficult, both because any curved walls could not easily be made to act as party walls, and because the pitched roofs would have caused drainage problems. In fact, virtually all of the curvilinear structures known are free-standing.[1]

The distinction between orthogonal and curvilinear houses is important in considering what they looked like and how their forms influenced the layout of a whole settlement. But this way of categorising them does not tell us much about how an individual house functioned to support the social lives of its inhabitants. A variety of other features are potentially more helpful for this purpose. Three basic aspects of the layout are particularly revealing. Most fundamental is the scale of the building. Cross-culturally this has been shown to relate to a variety of different factors including the size and wealth of the occupying household, and the economic system, which might require individual households to store sufficient foodstuffs to supply their own basic needs throughout the year. More relevant for present purposes, however, is the fact that scale is also linked with the type of social interaction which may have taken place between the occupants. This is because the amount of space available affects the range of tasks which could be undertaken inside and the number of activities which could be performed simultaneously. A second significant dimension is the degree to which interior space was subdivided into different rooms. The existence of internal walls would have meant that activities, and the individuals carrying them out, could have been separated physically, thus limiting social contact. Third, the number and arrangement of the doorways would also have played a key role: those between different interior rooms would have restricted or facilitated interaction between the occupants of different spaces, while those leading to the exterior would have channeled communication with the outside world. In short, these basic aspects of layout offer an indication of whether the occupants of a house could see and hear each other, and how easily they could communicate with those outside, as they carried out their daily activities. Hence they constitute important tools for investigating social relationships.

What, then, is the range of different types of layout found in Greek houses during the Early Iron Age? What do those layouts tell us about the social lives of the occupants of these houses? How similar or different

[1] Exceptions are an unexcavated apsidal structure at Oikonomos on Paros which seems to have had an rectilinear building constructed alongside it (Lang 1996, 184–5 with further references), and the oval structures from Lathouriza in Attica, which form a cluster, although the Lathouriza complex has been redated by Hans Lohmann to the Late Antique period (ibid. 21, n. 23 citing a personal communication).

were the day-to-day activities of families living in different parts of the Greek world and in different centuries? And what do those similarities and differences tell us about changes in domestic behaviour which may have been linked with the crystallisation of the citizen-state? These questions can be addressed by considering the different kinds of house plans in use and their frequencies at various points in time in different parts of the Greek world.

EARLY IRON AGE HOUSE-FORMS

Single-room structures (Figure 2.2)

Perhaps the most surprising observation to emerge from a quantitative approach to this material is that the vast majority of houses in the sample are single-room structures, which account for sixty-one examples, around half of the total (Figure 2.3). These were usually elongated in shape and could be either apsidal or rectangular. As a rule there was a single entrance on one of the short sides (in the context of apsidal buildings, this was at the opposite end from the apse). There is wide variation in floor area. The maximum interior living space known for a single-room house of this period is around 80 square metres, but about half of the structures of this type have a floor area of less than 30 square metres. The mean area ranges from 32 square metres at its lowest (during the sixth century) up to 42 square metres at its highest (during the eighth century).

The smallest of these buildings, such as the tenth century 'oval' house from Old Smyrna in Asia Minor (Akurgal 1983, 17–19), have an area of only around 10 square metres. In some instances the available interior space was supplemented by a porch area at the front, as in the eighth-century Lower Megaron at Emborio on the island of Chios, where the living area totalled about 60 square metres. This kind of porch is an important feature: not only would it have increased the amount of roofed space available, but it would also have acted as a transitional area between interior and exterior, providing a space which was lighter and better ventilated than the inside. Use also seems to have been made of exterior space, as suggested by the paved 'courtyard' area in front of the smaller structure adjacent to the Lower Megaron and House A at Emborio.

Little is known about how the main room would have been used in this kind of house. At Emborio, the Lower Megaron contained a hearth, while House A was provided with a raised bench along one side. It is rare to find a good range of artefacts preserved *in situ* which might reveal more about

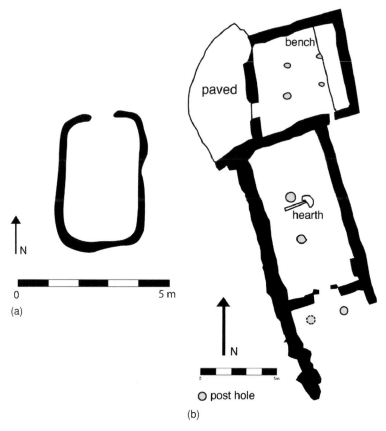

Figure 2.2 Plans of single-room houses: (a) the oval house at Old Smyrna; (b) the Lower Megaron (bottom) and House A at Emborio

the activities carried out in association with these features. The floor of the Lower Megaron yielded only fragments of a pitcher and jug along with a fragmentary courseware vessel, while no artefacts at all seem to have been found on the floor of House A. At Smyrna the only finds listed as associated with the floor level are an amphora and a krater (vessels used for storing and mixing liquids such as water and wine), and their locations within the structure are not noted in the publication (Akurgal 1983, 18).

At other sites information about objects found is generally more limited, but the amount of variability in house size alone suggests that there are likely to have been considerable differences between structures, both in the way in which interior space was used, and perhaps also in the number

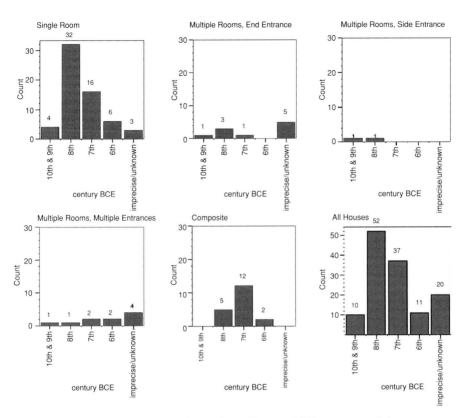

Figure 2.3 Graphs showing the numbers of houses of different types and dates in the sample

of individuals using it. The smallest buildings, such as the Smyrna house, would have been quite cramped, and for this reason it is likely that interior space would perhaps have been used flexibly, with different activities taking place in the same area at different times. Somewhat surprisingly, perhaps, these smaller houses tend to lack the kind of formal exterior court identified at Emborio, but it is still possible that some domestic activities took place outside. A floor area of around 10 square metres roughly equates to that shown by ethnographic study to be the amount of space habitually occupied by a single individual, or at most a couple, in societies where groups live in compounds consisting of small, one- or two-person, dwellings (Flannery 1972, 31). Obviously this does not mean that houses of this size were necessarily occupied only by such small numbers of people. But it does underline how cramped some of the Greek structures were, and the possibility cannot be discounted that some of them actually represent parts of larger dwelling compounds consisting of several separate build-ings which functioned as a single residential complex (as has recently been argued by Alexander Mazarakis Ainian: Mazarakis Ainian 2007).

Even in the larger buildings, the lack of interior divisions would have had implications for the daily lives of the occupants. Anyone entering or leaving the building, and all of the activities taking place here, would have been visible to everyone else present, so there would have been no 'privacy' in the way we understand the term. In a number of contemporary societies where single-room houses are common, however, interior space is used differentially even without fixed boundaries demarcating separate areas, and the same may have been true in Early Iron Age Greece. It is also possible that some temporary or lightweight dividers were in place which have left scant trace in the archaeological record.[2]

Although these single-room structures could reach a considerable size, there is also an unsurprising tendency for larger houses to be subdivided, the average size of the rooms increasing with the size of the building (Figure 2.4). Based on differences in their circulation patterns, four forms of multiple-room house can be distinguished: those with multiple rooms and a single entrance at one end; those with multiple rooms and a single entrance located along one side; those with multiple rooms and multiple entrances; and a composite form consisting of clusters of rooms. These various arrangements would have had different implications for patterns of social interaction between their occupants.

Multiple-room structures with end entrance (Figure 2.5)

One approach to laying out a house with several rooms was to build a version of the elongated, single-room structure with entrance on the short side, but to divide it crosswise with partition walls. This layout is most common in central Greece during the ninth and eighth centuries, and appears to die out after the seventh century, although some examples cannot be closely dated. A well-known example, Unit IV.1 at Nichoria, which dates to the tenth and ninth centuries BCE, is fairly typical in layout: the entrance is on one of the short sides, sheltered by a porch. This leads into a large main room which gives in turn onto a smaller space in an apse at

---

[2] A row of flat stones found in the apse of the eighth-century house, Unit IV.5 at Nichoria, has been suggested as possible evidence of some sort of lightweight room divider of this type (Coulson 1983, 50).

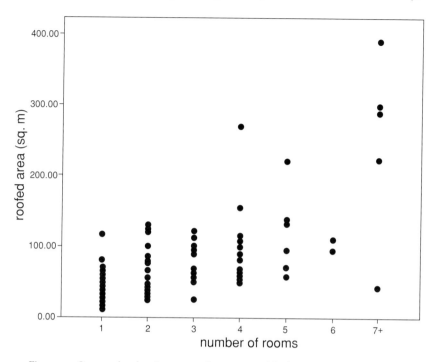

Figure 2.4 Scatter-plot showing range of areas covered by houses in the sample with different numbers of rooms

the other end of the building.[3] The second phase of the structure, dating to the later ninth century, offers unusually detailed information about some of the domestic activities carried out and about how these were organised within the available space. A major feature in the main room was a circular masonry platform. Fragments of animal bones, table pottery and drinking vessels found around it suggest that eating and drinking took place here. A hearth near the centre of the room may have been used for cooking. Further fragments of table vessels in the porch seem to indicate that this was also a location for eating and drinking, although we cannot tell whether it was used at different times of day, during different seasons, or by different individuals, from the hearth area. Spindle whorls found in the main room indicate the use or storage of equipment for producing cloth. The apse

[3] In an early phase of the building's history the apse may have been accessible directly from the exterior via a second entrance (Mazarakis Ainian 1992, 76, 80 and Figure 4), although in its later phase the main door on the short side seems to have been the only means of access to the building. It is this later phase which is discussed here.

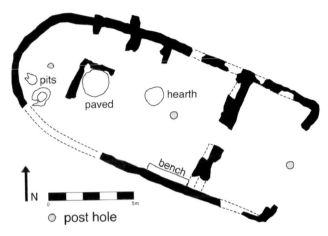

Figure 2.5 Plan of a multiple-room house with end entrance: Unit IV.1 at Nichoria

room yielded two pits containing stored legumes together with a diverse array of items such as an axe and a shield boss. The two rooms of the house may therefore have been used for different purposes, and within the single large hearth room there may have been some degree of differentiation in the way in which space was used, with cooking towards the door and food consumption further back around the large circular platform.

The absence of corridors in Unit IV.1 and other houses of this type would have meant that at any one time only the individuals using the end room would have remained unobserved and uninterrupted by others entering the house or moving around to undertake various domestic tasks. Like the complete absence of partitions in the single-room houses, this suggests that privacy, in the modern western sense of the word, was not a priority in these households.

Houses with multiple rooms and a side entrance (Figure 2.6)

An alternative to locating the main entrance on one of the short ends of the building was to put it at the centre of one of the long sides. This pattern is rarely found, occurring only in Crete and western Greece, and only between the tenth and eighth centuries. Building A at Kavousi Kastro, on Crete, is an example. Although superficially similar to the previous arrangement, the different location of the doorway alters the pattern of circulation. The excavators identify the main entrance as a door in room

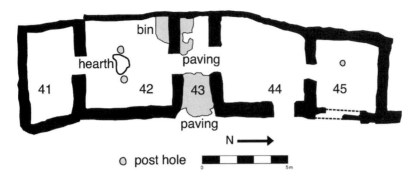

Figure 2.6 Plan of a multiple-room house with side entrance: House A at Kavousi Kastro

44 (Coulson *et al.* 1997, 319), although for at least part of the life of the house the adjacent space 43 was also entered from the exterior (Coulson *et al.* 1997, 323–324). From 43 and 44 it was possible to move, in the first phase of occupation, either northwards into room 45, or southwards to 42 and through it to 41.

Detailed information about the architectural features and the finds, which most probably date from the final phase of the building's use, during the later seventh century BCE, led the excavators to suggest some of the ways in which the individual spaces may have functioned. A paved floor in 43 suggests that it may have been unroofed. A built oven here was accompanied by a range of finds including querns, pot-stands and drinking cups which may indicate that food preparation took place in this area. Rooms 42, 44 and 45 together contained pithoi (storage jars) and a variety of stone features such as benches and bins which were probably also used for storage. A built hearth and finds of drinking vessels and loom weights in 42 may suggest that other domestic tasks were also carried out here (Coulson *et al.* 1997, 320–326).

The most isolated room in terms of its position in the house is room 41, which lies at the southern end of the house and could be closed off with a door (Coulson *et al.* 1997, 329). Inside were a further hearth and a few finds including a number of drinking cups. The excavators interpret the room as a sleeping area, but this depends on two a priori assumptions: first, that a specialised space was provided for this purpose, and second, that sleeping was considered to be an activity requiring visual privacy, neither of which is argued for in their discussion. It seems wiser to note that the room seems to lack the food storage and/or preparation vessels seen in most of the other areas of the house, and that it may have been used for activities requiring seclusion from the remainder of the household, including – if the cups represent usage rather than storage patterns – for drinking.

In the Kavousi building and others like it, the position of the door to the exterior in a central room, rather than at one end, would have increased from one to two the number of rooms which had no through traffic. It would also have meant that in order to reach a specific room an individual would have had to move through fewer intervening ones. The arrival of visitors might therefore have caused less disruption, and the number of areas in which seclusion might be guaranteed would have been increased. At the same time the reduced number of rooms receding from each entrance would have enabled more daylight to penetrate the interior than in the houses with end entrances, providing better lighting and ventilation. Some of these advantages would have been lost in the later of the two occupation phases, however, when, in common with other structures at the site, the house appears to have been reduced in size, with room 45 walled off from the remainder of the structure.

Multiple-room structures with more than one entrance (Figure 2.7)

A further organisational scheme involved the creation of a series of separate entrances from the exterior which led to different spaces. Two arrangements are found. The more common pattern consists of a cluster of rooms each with its own door, all opening into a central area. This is the form adopted by houses of the Classical and Hellenistic periods, where the central space is an open court (see Chapter 3). Structures of this type first appear in the eighth century, and during the period discussed here no examples are found outside central Greece. Some of these buildings have been the subject of conflicting interpretations and they may not all have been primarily residential in function.[4] Examples which do seem certain to have played a domestic role include the houses from Vroulia on Rhodes. One of the better-preserved units at the site is 22–23, which may together constitute a single residential complex. It is noteworthy that while the inner and outer doorways in 22 are roughly aligned, those in 23 deliberately seem to have been offset. Such an arrangement would have made the inner room dark (any form of window opening onto the outside is unlikely, given that the structure was part of a terrace with rooms on either side, and

---

[4] Examples include the well-known building F from the Athenian Agora, which has been identified as a Peisistratid palace or a public building: Boersma 2000, 54–55 with further references.

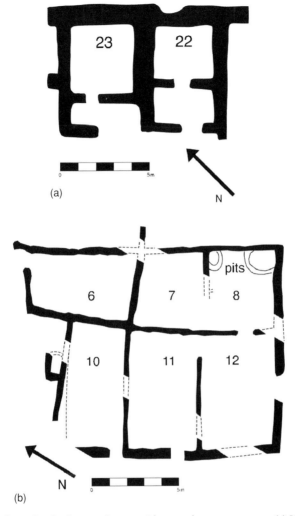

Figure 2.7 Plans of multiple-room houses with more than one entrance: (a) Unit 22–23 at Vroulia; (b) level 9 structure at Kastanas

was built up against a fortification wall at the rear). Indeed fragments of a lamp are reported to have been found here (Kinch 1914, 159). Such an arrangement may indicate a desire to create an isolated space in the back room of 23, although no other finds are recorded and the precise function of the room is therefore unclear. Elsewhere in the complex, further items offer a picture of various domestic activities: in room 22 some large pithoi suggest storage of agricultural produce. A cooking vessel, a cup and a large fine-ware container were also found here.

A second, rather uncommon, form of multiple-room house consists of a block of rooms in which the entrances face outwards in different directions rather than inwards onto a single common area. Such structures are difficult to interpret since, unless there is evidence for connecting doors, it is not always obvious whether the individual cells represent the rooms of a single residence or constitute a series of separate dwellings with fewer rooms. This problem is exemplified by the so-called central house in the earliest Geometric level from the tell site of Kastanas in Greek Macedonia. The excavators interpret this block as constituting a single dwelling although it had numerous external doorways and non-connecting units. Their interpretation rests on the fact that the block seems to have been planned and constructed in one operation, and that the finds and features seem to indicate that the various spaces played complementary roles. In fact, however, there are other sites of this period where party walls are shared between houses (for example Zagora on Andros, discussed in the next section). At the same time, there is also some overlap in the functions of the rooms suggested by the finds, with much of the interior space being devoted to storage. For example, rooms 11 and 12, which were at the front and entered separately from the exterior, both contained cooking- and coarse-wares and were therefore probably used for food preparation and/or storage.

Even if the individual blocks of this type of house do represent a larger number of individual dwellings, however, the implications of the con-figuration remain similar. In both the Vroulia and Kastanas types the arrangement of space would have offered some scope for separating dif-ferent activities and would have enabled individuals to use certain rooms undisturbed because the lack of communicating doors would have elim-inated through traffic. The use of offset entrances for some spaces, as at Vroulia, would have enhanced the potential for isolating these spaces by eliminating any possibility of a view through the house even if doors were left open to provide some light and ventilation.

Composite houses (Figure 2.8)

There were, then, a variety of different solutions to the problem of creating a multi-room house, each of which had different implications in terms of the patterns of activity and social relationships which it could have supported. In practice, at a single settlement, and even sometimes within

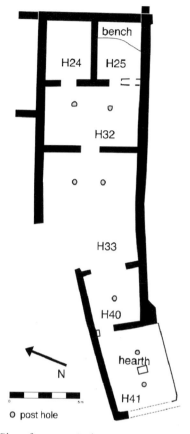

Figure 2.8 Plan of a composite house: House 24/25/32 at Zagora

a single building, a combination of different strategies was frequently employed, creating a composite structure. An illustration of this is to be found in the complex houses at Zagora on Andros (Cambitoglou *et al.* 1971; Cambitoglou *et al.* 1988), which are often cited as examples of Greek Early Iron Age houses. The site was inhabited for much of the eighth century and the excavators were able to identify two separate occupation phases. Adaptations of the architecture during the second phase suggest that the original roofed area of each residential unit was subsequently augmented, a change which was associated with new patterns of activity. Similar alterations seem to have been made to a number of different houses. An example is Unit H24/25/32/33, where an original large room was divided into three smaller ones, one of which contained a bench. Finds from two of these suggest that most, or all, of this complex was devoted to storage, and the bench seems, like benches elsewhere at the site, to have been used as a stand for pottery vessels. The house was extended by the construction of a new unit, H40/41, which lay on the opposite side of an open court, H33. H41, an inner room with a hearth, was approached through a smaller, outer, room (H40) which had a broad doorway opening to the court. Finds of pottery associated with this second occupation phase suggest that the original nucleus of the building was now used mainly for storage, while the new rooms served for preparation and consumption of food.

In essence, the Zagora houses represent a complex version of the house with multiple rooms and multiple entrances leading off a single space. But the use of two-room units would have meant that the outer rooms would have been subject to through traffic, and created fewer secluded spaces than a house with a comparable number of rooms where each was entered individually. In interpreting the Zagora houses and assessing their social significance, great importance has sometimes been attached to the presence of the courtyard, which in some cases seems to have been enclosed between the surrounding house walls, an arrangement that has been taken to imply a need to restrict access from the exterior (Morris 2000, 285–286). The court is potentially significant since it would have extended the space available for domestic activities, at least in the warmer summer months. A formally demarcated exterior activity area is also something found in connection with some other houses of this period, although there is no evidence that in those cases they were deliberately enclosed or screened from view.[5] The few instances at Zagora where the court does appear to be fully enclosed thus seem anomalous, and rather than being deliberate, they may well have resulted from the process by which the site as a whole developed. Placing additional units on the other side of an open court enabled an expansion of the roofed area of an existing structure while still maintaining access, light and air for the original part of the house. Such an arrangement may also have retained an existing open-air activity area in the same location.

Composite houses like those at Zagora provided flexible structures which could be expanded to accommodate changes in requirements for household space, whether those were caused by growth in the number of occupants or by underlying change in patterns of domestic activity. While additional units could be used to increase existing living space, the subdivision of those same units would have enabled physical separation of different activity

---

[5] At Kavousi Kastro, for instance, it has been suggested that such areas sometimes began as sections of street (Preston-Day 1990, 181).

areas. Although it would have been necessary to pass through the front area of each unit in order to reach the back room, the unitary form itself must have limited the amount of through traffic and helped to create spaces which were more secluded than, for example, those of structures such as Nichoria Unit IV.1 and other, larger, buildings with this design.

SUMMARISING THE ARCHAEOLOGICAL EVIDENCE

In terms of its geographical distribution, the majority of the evidence for Early Iron Age housing comes from central Greece. (See Figure 2.9. The pattern also holds true if the number of sites, rather than the number of houses, in each region is compared.) One explanation may be that this represents an area which is very thoroughly explored and where the houses are likely to be relatively close to the modern land surface (as opposed to, for example, the more deeply buried structures characteristic of tell sites in northern Greece). Nevertheless, the scale of the difference, together with the fact that the region is relatively small, suggests that at least part of it may have been more densely inhabited than other areas. Within central Greece the most striking finding is that single-room houses predominated throughout the period between the tenth and sixth centuries. The eighth century, which has often been regarded as a time of rapid change, saw a sudden and dramatic increase both in the number of houses known and in the number of sites from which evidence for housing can be studied. This phenomenon coincides with the timing of the 'structural revolution' identified by Anthony Snodgrass on the basis of a wide range of different types of archaeological material (Snodgrass 1980), and might be seen as supporting his proposal that there was a significant increase in population during this period albeit less extreme than he originally argued. Simultaneously, small numbers of two new types of layout appeared – the composite house and the multiple-room house with multiple entrances into a central space. The pattern is not one of steady change, however, since the number of examples of both these types seem to have peaked in the seventh century and dropped back again during the sixth.

By contrast with central Greece, numbers of excavated houses are too small in western Greece, northern Greece and Crete to offer a detailed picture of how the syntax of domestic space in these areas may have changed through time. If we take a synchronic view of these areas, however, it is clear that there are regional preferences for different patterns of domestic organisation: multiple-room houses with multiple outward-facing entrances are only found in northern Greece, while multiple-room houses with a single

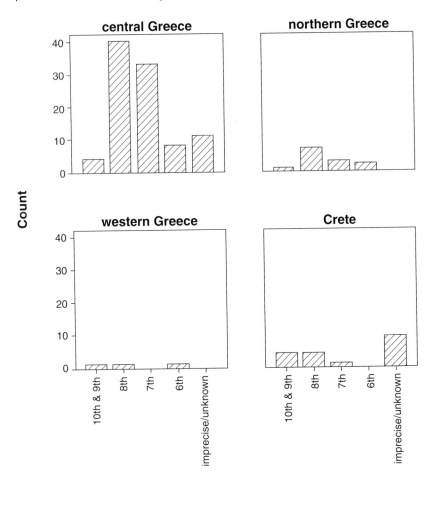

Figure 2.9 Graph showing the numbers of houses in the sample from the different geographical regions

entrance on the side are found only on Crete. These patterns in the organisation of domestic space reinforce the impression of regionalism seen in other types of archaeological evidence from this period.

Where details of the finds and features of the different house types can be studied, they provide evidence only for a limited number of activities.

The most easily identifiable is storage, which frequently took place in several different areas within a single structure. Fine wares associated with consumption of food and drink tend to have a slightly narrower pattern of distribution, often occurring together and in conjunction with hearths. At Kavousi Kastro and Kastanas the occurrence of drinking vessels alone, in inner rooms which would have been relatively secluded, may suggest a significant difference in the spatial location of eating and drinking together, as opposed to drinking without food. If the inner rooms were preferred for drinking, we might be seeing the emergence of one of the elements which has been viewed as characteristic of the later symposium or drinking party (discussed in detail in Chapter 3), namely the use of an enclosed space which is separated from the remainder of the household. Its appearance in houses in Crete and northern Greece would represent an interesting phenomenon, given that culturally these areas seem to have been significantly different from central Greece which has been the focus of studies of the later period. In contrast with food storage and consumption, artefacts associated with food preparation are normally concentrated in a single area which is often close to the main entrance – possibly in order to make the most of light entering through an open door, and in some cases enabling smoke from a cooking fire or brazier to escape.

A further aspect of this material is also worth considering, and that is the chronological distribution of sites. With the exception of a few isolated examples, most of the Dark Age and Archaic structures are not located in settlements which subsequently became major city states, but on small sites, most of which had been abandoned by the Classical period. It is therefore possible that at least some of these structures followed different trajectories from those at sites which did go on to become citizen-states. This may be one reason why the sample size for the sixth century is relatively small: much of the evidence for domestic organisation at this date may have been destroyed by later phases at major sites such as Athens and Corinth. The apparent reversion to eighth-century patterns during the sixth century may therefore be illusory, resulting from a bias in our sample which means that the smaller, more backward looking, sites are the main evidence to have survived.

CONCLUSION: DOMESTIC ORGANISATION AND THE FORMATION OF THE CITIZEN-STATE

The picture, then, is a fragmentary one: from the eighth century there is a gradual trend towards the increasing segmentation of space, indicating increasing complexity in social relations. But change seems to have been gradual and to some extent non-linear. At the same time it followed different pathways at different sites and in different regions, with residential structures changing in a variety of ways. By the eighth century, architectural devices were already beginning to appear which could potentially be used to control circulation, for example a single outside door or a space giving access to several individual rooms. But overall there do not appear to have been consistent attempts to separate individuals within the domestic context or to control their movement since the majority of structures had only a single room, and even those which were subdivided often required their occupants to move through one room in order to reach another, thereby affording little in the way of spatial separation. This seems to indicate that, even in the sixth century, it was not felt necessary to conform to the specific patterns of architecture and spatial organisation which seem to be characteristic of Classical citizen-states. Such a conclusion fits with the Athenian textual sources, which suggest that citizenship there was only formally circumscribed during the fifth century, with Pericles' citizenship law, which defined citizenship based on parentage. This may have been the point at which a need arose to control contact between women and unrelated men so that a householder could be seen to be securing the parentage of his offspring.

CHAPTER 3

A space for 'hurling the furniture'? Architecture and the development of Greek domestic symposia

I only mix three rounds of wine for moderate men – one for health, which they drink first, a second one for love and enjoyment, and a third for sleep. Sensible visitors go home when this one is finished. The fourth round is out of control and is ruled by violence; the fifth one by commotion, the sixth by drunken rowdiness, the seventh one leads to black eyes. The eighth round belongs to the police, the ninth to nausea, and the tenth to craziness and hurling the furniture.

Euboulos, quoted in Athenaeus, Deipnosophistae 2.36b

How space, time and people are organized is not random. The organization interrelates with deeper concepts of social values concerning gender relations, age relations and other forms of status relations, as well as more abstract values such as beliefs about privacy and community...

Pader 1997, 72

INTRODUCTION

In Chapter 2 I suggested that the close association between the scale and layout of a house and the complexity of the society to which its inhabitants belonged offers a new perspective through which to explore the formation of the Greek polis or citizen-state. This chapter focuses on the development of one of the social institutions which were instrumental in structuring relationships within the polis, namely the symposium or drinking party (Small 1997, 113). Discussion of the symposium has tended to focus on ancient texts and on painted pottery which appears to show such occasions in progress, but, although it is assumed that they were frequently held in private houses and that the architectural setting played an important role in shaping the atmosphere, little attention has been paid to the archaeological evidence of housing as a source for understanding sympotic behaviour. My goal here is therefore to examine the architecture and organisation of spaces which may have been used for the domestic symposium, in order to explore aspects of its history and the role that it may have played in relation to some of the other dimensions of domestic and civic social life.

The symposium has traditionally been viewed by modern scholars as a cultural 'package' which was defined by the observance of a number of different conventions. These include: serving little if any food, so that the focus was on wine and on accompanying conversation and entertainment; the reclining position of participants, who lay two to a couch; the possible participation of unrelated female entertainers, and simultaneous exclusion of respectable women (the wives and daughters of citizen men); and the spatial isolation of the drinkers, which enabled transgression of normal social rules and the foregrounding of humour and sexuality.[1] While there is already evidence for social eating and drinking in the Late Bronze Age and in some Early Iron Age communities, and for reclining banquets in the Near East during the same period, the stage at which this specific set of elements came together in the Greek world is difficult to assess. The most explicit and detailed evidence for them comes from textual sources dating to the fifth and fourth centuries BCE, but there is also more indirect support for a somewhat earlier date: some of the lyric poetry of the Archaic period is interpreted as showing a spirit appropriate to a sympotic context, and therefore as having been performed at such occasions. In addition representations of drinkers reclining on couches are found on ceramic vessels from the start of the sixth century. Some scholars have tried to push the evidence back further, arguing that the symposium can already be detected in Greek communities as early as the eighth century BCE, when cups assumed to have been used for wine are found at numerous settlement sites. One such vessel, commonly referred to as 'Nestor's cup', was found in a child's grave on the island of Ischia, off the coast of southern Italy. It bears one of the earliest known examples of alphabetic Greek script, three lines of verse incised onto the exterior which are reminiscent of the Archaic lyric performance pieces and have been used to support the identification of such cups with sympotic behaviour (Murray 1994).

This long history raises the possibility of change through time in sympotic practice: in particular it has been suggested that contrasting social groups may have taken part during different periods. Like 'Nestor's cup', many of the early finds of drinking cups come not from mainland Greece

---

[1] This definition emerges particularly from the work of Oswyn Murray (for example Murray 1983, Murray 1990, Murray 2003) although most of these elements are also stressed individually by other scholars. I use the expression 'domestic symposium' here to distinguish this from any similar occasions which may have been held in civic or religious settings.

but from Greek communities in the eastern and western Mediterranean, raising the possibility that the origins of the practice lay with merchants or traders. During the Archaic period, it is suggested, the symposium became an occasion participated in by the aristocracy, serving to build alliances between elite families and to bolster aristocratic power. Indeed, some scholars have even argued that during this period politics were conducted only through activities like the symposium and that there was no separate political sphere (Schmitt-Pantel 1990b). The role of the symposium during the fifth and fourth centuries has similarly been debated, with some arguing that it remained an elite activity and was a focus for anti-democratic sentiment, while others see it as an occasion in which large numbers of men of citizen status would have participated. To what extent, then, does the architectural evidence support these ideas about the origins and development of the domestic symposium? What can it tell us about the status of the individuals involved? And what does it reveal about the role played by the symposium in relation to other kinds of social drinking? In order to address these questions I want to begin by exploring the architectural setting for the Classical symposium and try to trace its different features backwards in time.

LOCATING THE SYMPOSIUM IN THE DOMESTIC CONTEXT: THE FIFTH AND FOURTH CENTURIES BCE

Remains of houses of later fifth- and fourth-century date at numerous archaeological sites offer convincing evidence for a physical setting in which the symposium, as outlined above, could have taken place. The most extensively excavated site is the city of Olynthus in the Chalcidici, where more than fifty houses have been completely explored in a large residential area (the so-called North Hill). This part of the city was laid out at around 400 BCE and destroyed in 348 BCE after being besieged and captured by Philip II of Macedon. The houses themselves were therefore occupied during a relatively short period. While individual properties vary somewhat in size and layout, all but the smallest are organised on the same basic plan which shares similarities with houses found in many other parts of the Greek world, including at Athens. An individual structure occupied around 290 square metres in ground area and consisted of around ten rooms on the ground floor, space which was often supplemented by further apartments in an upper storey. The house as a whole is inward-looking and centred around an open court at the centre or south of the building (Figure 3.1). There is strict separation from the street. Each house was

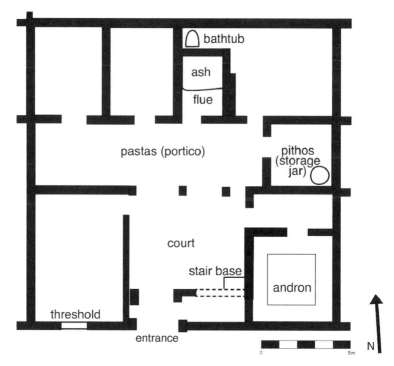

Figure 3.1 Plan of an example of a Classical courtyard house: Olynthus House Avii4

normally entered via a single street door. (More rarely, a second street door opened into a large room facing onto the street, as in Figure 3.1, which did not typically communicate with the main part of the house.) Even when the street door was open, in most cases a passer-by would have been prevented from catching a glimpse of the interior by a second, inner, door, a screen wall or by a winding corridor immediately beyond the doorway. Once inside, however, a visitor would generally have passed through into an open interior courtyard and would have seen the entrances to around ten different rooms leading off here and off an adjacent portico. In addition there was frequently a staircase leading to an upper-storey gallery which looked down onto the court and gave access to further accommodation above some of the ground floor rooms. Even during the day, the interior of the house would have been dark and difficult to see into since large windows seem not to have been used: on analogy with better-preserved houses elsewhere, the doorway into the courtyard or portico was probably the main source of daylight, and the only openings in the walls are likely to have been small and located high up in the wall, providing ventilation rather than light.

Although these properties were relatively spacious, furnishing was sparse in comparison with modern homes. As in the Early Iron Age and Archaic structures discussed in Chapter 2, most of the rooms had beaten earth floors with mud-brick walls. Some of the few built-in features were also similar, with large sunken jars and hearths attesting to the storage and preparation of food. At the same time, there were also a few more amenities: for example, a well or cistern in the courtyard often provided a source of water, and supplies drawn from here could be poured into a terracotta hip bath for washing and then emptied into a system of terracotta drains which ran beneath the house and opened into a communal drainage system under the street outside. There would also have been some items of wooden furniture which no longer survive. These would have included tables, couches, chairs or stools, and storage chests, all of which can be traced through their metal components such as nails, bosses, hinges and other fittings. Other furnishings such as patterned textiles may also have added to the comfort of some rooms, although they are no longer preserved.

Many of the interior apartments of these houses lack surviving architectural features to suggest how they might have been used. Nevertheless, at Olynthus and at other sites of late fifth- and fourth-century date, some do preserve one distinctively furnished room which has convincingly been interpreted as an andron, a space serving as a setting for the symposium (although it may have been used in other ways as well). This takes the form of a square chamber with an off-centre doorway and raised or marked borders running along the edges of the floor (Plate 3.1). In contrast with most of the remainder of the house the walls here frequently feature decorative panels of red or yellow plaster. The floor was mortar, sometimes with inlaid mosaic decoration at the centre, while the border was normally left undecorated. At Olynthus the mosaics were composed of pebbles laid in geometric patterns or depicting images from myth. In later houses specially cut stone cubes (known as tesserae) were used to create more intricate designs. The off-centre doorway and raised or plain borders on the floor would have accommodated a continuous line of the couches on which participants reclined at a symposium. Smaller androns had space for three couches, while in the larger rooms five or seven were accommodated, the latter making the room suitable for parties of up to fourteen. The open space at the centre of the room would have been used for serving the guests and in the larger examples perhaps also as a space for musical or dance performances (Smith 2000).

Plate 3.1 View of an andron showing marked border, off-centre doorway and mosaic floor: House AV6 at Olynthus

As well as making the room more pleasant, the wall and floor decoration seems designed to enhance the household's prestige by demonstrating the wealth and good taste of the owner. Indeed, in some communities the presence and location of the andron is also signalled on the exterior of the house by the incorporation of masonry of higher quality than that used for the walls of the neighbouring rooms – a feature which suggests that possession of an andron played a symbolic as well as a practical role, and that its architecture was used to communicate with passers-by in the street as well as with guests entering the property (Nevett 2009b). In many cases an anteroom, decorated in a similar manner to the andron, provided a degree of separation from the remainder of the house. Even where an anteroom was not present, substantial threshold blocks with fittings for hinges indicate that heavy doors were present which could potentially be used to close off the andron. These features suggest that some of the activities taking place inside this room required some isolation or distance from the remainder of the household.

Scholars have often thought of Greek culture as polarised between the civic arena of the male citizens and the domestic sphere which was associated with their wives, but the domestic symposium is one of several practices which highlight the inadequacy of this distinction, in this case by placing a key masculine activity at the heart of the house. The apparent paradox has often been explained by suggesting that male and female members of Greek households habitually occupied different sets of domestic apartments, with women's space consisting of upper storeys and inner areas where domestic chores were carried out. In fact, the organisation of household space itself demonstrates that domestic social relationships were rather more complex (Nevett 1999). In most cases the andron is reached from the central courtyard, just like the other rooms, and those rooms rarely communicate with each other directly so that it would have been necessary to walk through the courtyard or portico in order to move between them.[2] The artefacts found in such courtyard areas, both at Olynthus and at other sites of similar date, suggest that a variety of domestic activities took place here including storage and preparation of food.

To judge by textual sources, such activities may have been performed, or at least supervised, by the female relatives of the house-owner. It is likely, then, that male and female members of the household regularly used the same spaces and encountered each other in the course of their daily activities. But the women of the household could have been prevented from meeting male guests coming through the court on their way to the andron if social conventions were in operation requiring that activity in the courtyard area would have ceased and those involved would have withdrawn to one of the interior rooms when visitors were present – as in certain traditional Islamic societies when male visitors enter a house (compare Nevett 1994). The location of the andron alongside the other domestic quarters suggests that any such need for separation between the two sexes was only temporary, while the organisation of space in the house as a whole implies that for most of the time there would have been frequent contact between the different members of the household as they worked in the courtyard area or moved from room to room. When not in use for a symposium the andron itself may perhaps also have served as a living room or for some other purpose, so that locating the entrance here rather than separating it from the remainder of the house may have made practical sense. At a symbolic level, the juxtaposition of andron and domestic quarters may also

---

[2] There are a handful of examples of houses which are split into two separate areas, an inner courtyard around which domestic activities such as food preparation took place, and an outer court around which an andron and other living spaces were located, including several houses at Eretria and a house at Maroneia in Greek Thrace (see Nevett 1999, 107–114 with further references). This pattern of organisation seems to be unusual, however.

have represented a reminder of the overall power of the male householder over his household.

For the later fifth and fourth centuries, then, there is clear evidence in many houses for a room which would have been suited to the symposium in a variety of ways: there was provision for couches on which participants could have reclined, a degree of isolation from the remainder of the house-hold once guests were inside, and decoration which would have presented a good impression to visitors. To what extent do earlier houses yield evidence of comparable facilities which could have accommodated symposia?

LOCATING THE SYMPOSIUM IN PRE-CLASSICAL HOUSES

Identifying examples of andrones in earlier contexts is more challenging. For the period immediately prior to the later fifth century, examples of excavated houses are fewer. Where they have been investigated, the indi-vidual blocks of houses are frequently more irregular in form and therefore more difficult to interpret than later structures. For example, although the excavators of Olynthus' North Hill also explored a second, earlier, hous-ing area (the so-called South Hill), relatively few conclusions were drawn about the nature of the buildings here and no andrones were identified. In addition, mosaic floors which are one of the most durable and distinc-tive indicators of an andron are not found much before 400 BCE, so that locations for couches are difficult to identify in earlier contexts. Neverthe-less, some attempts have still been made to pinpoint spaces used for social drinking, even where such architectural clues are lacking.

In houses like those from the North Hill at Olynthus where the andron floor was composed of mortar or mosaic, this floor often seems to have been swept clean before the house was abandoned so that few artefacts were found. However, the beaten earth floors of the remainder the rooms, and those of earlier houses, often preserve fragments of pottery and other small artefacts which have been incorporated into the floor matrix and offer an idea of some of the types of objects which may have been used and/or stored in the room. At a few relevant sites where detailed study of the distribution of artefacts has been published there is clear evidence for drinking in domestic contexts from an early date: for example, in Unit IV.I at Nichoria in the Peloponnese (discussed in Chapter 2), a two-room house occupied during the tenth and ninth centuries BCE, pottery associated with drinking is concentrated around a circular masonry platform in the main room. There is, however, no evidence that the drinkers reclined, and consumption took place in one part of a larger space, in full view of the

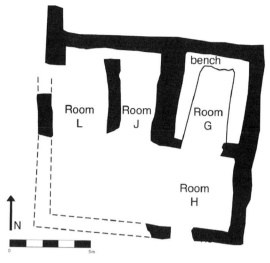

Figure 3.2 Plan of the eighth-century BCE house at Thorikos, Attica

other occupants of the house. This, together with the fact that alongside the drinking vessels there were plates and dishes for food consumption, suggests that activities taking place here were more likely to have been the kind of feasting which has been identified in other Early Iron Age contexts, rather than something which would have resembled a symposium in its narrow sense.

While the kind of communal eating and drinking suggested by the Nichoria material may well have been common in the Early Iron Age (compare, for example, Mazarakis Ainian 1997, 394), there are a few locations in which some scholars have identified specialised andrones which might indicate that symposia took place. One of the earliest is in a house at Thorikos in Attica which dates to the eighth century BCE (Bingen 1967). The building is not fully preserved but there seem to have been a total of only four spaces covering an area of around 50 square metres, about one sixth of the area of most of the Classical houses at Olynthus (Figure 3.2). One of these spaces, a narrow room, g, in the north-east corner, has been identified as an andron based on a raised bench feature running round three sides, which is compared with the plain or raised strip of flooring running around the edges of Classical andrones (Fusaro 1982, 10). Nevertheless, in this case the feature is irregular and in places is only 30cm wide, which seems too narrow to accommodate a couch or a man reclining. Even if this room were somehow used for drinking, its long and thin shape would

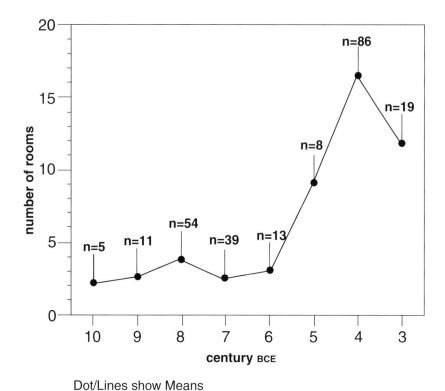

Dot/Lines show Means

Figure 3.3 Graphs showing change through time in mean house area and (overleaf) in
mean numbers of rooms per house

have created a different social dynamic from the later, square, andron of
the Classical period. In fact it seems preferable to interpret the room as a
storage area with raised surfaces on which jars may have been set, as seems
to have been the practice at another eighth-century BCE site, Zagora on
Andros (for example Cambitoglou *et al.* 1971, 18).

Another early site where androns have been identified is Vroulia on
Rhodes, where a series of adjoining residential buildings were in use during
the late seventh to early sixth century. Again, one room in each complex
is identified as an andron based on a similar stone ledge running along
the walls. As at Thorikos, this is also too narrow to accommodate a man
reclining, which has led to the suggestion that the occupants would have
sat rather than reclined (Hoepfner 1999, 197). Again, even if it is correct
to identify these rooms as specialised androns, this interpretation would
still alter one of the features of the symposium seen as most characteristic,

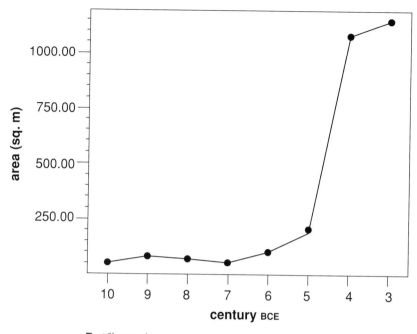

area (sq. m)

century BCE

Dot/lines show means

Figure 3.3 (*cont.*)

namely the reclining posture of the drinkers, and again the atmosphere of the occasion taking place in such rooms would have been fundamentally different from that envisaged for the Classical symposium.

The difficulty in finding an Archaic house equipped with a space equivalent to the later andron is brought out by looking at how house size and spatial organisation more generally changed through time at a large number of sites. Comparison between housing at a sample of Classical and Hellenistic sites and the evidence for Early Iron Age housing considered in Chapter 2 reveals some interesting changes in the way in which domestic space was configured.[3] At the beginning of this period the majority of houses were relatively small, comprising two or three rooms and covering a mean area of *c*. 50 square metres (Figure 3.3). The main functional divisions seem to have been between spaces which the associated finds suggest were used for living, for food preparation and for storage. Evidence for the sixth

---

[3] While this group of data may well not be absolutely representative of all the housing of each century, the trends emerging are sufficiently clear and consistent to suggest that they offer a reliable indication of the kinds of changes taking place.

century is limited, making it difficult to generalise, but during the fifth century many more examples of houses are known (most of them dating towards the end of the century). By this time mean area has increased to 170 square metres, with the available living space augmented further in some cases by the use of upper storeys. At the same time the mean number of rooms on the ground floor of each property is nine, giving a mean room area of 17 square metres. It is at this point that we see the emergence, alongside the functional areas such as stores and cooking facilities, of clear examples of the kinds of androns described above, with their off-centre doorways and borders for couches. A parallel move away from the sequential arrangement of spaces seen in the Early Iron Age, to the radial, courtyard layout, also offers more scope for providing the kind of enclosed atmosphere removed from the outside world which has been envisioned as such a vital element of the symposium.

Although the radially planned Classical houses are generally larger than their Early Iron Age predecessors and offered more amenities, they do retain one of the major characteristics of the earlier structures, namely a pattern of organisation which would have brought the different users of the house into close contact with each other. In the earlier buildings this resulted from limitations on amount of available space and the fact that the interior was divided into only a small number of rooms which were arranged in such a way that it would have been necessary to pass through one in order to reach the next. In the Classical courtyard house, although there was more space and a greater number of rooms, the radial pattern of organisation and the necessity of passing through the court to move between those rooms or to enter or leave the house would have created a similar effect: the various household members would have known each other's movements even if they were occupying separate spaces. Thus, the presence in the courtyard of visitors en route to or from the andron would have been clear to the inhabitants of other interior rooms, although they themselves could have remained unobserved within the dark interior. Similarly the movements of slaves or servants into and around the house (accessing storerooms, for example) could easily have been monitored by the house-owner or his wife, and indeed husband and/or wife could have been kept under observation by each other or by other members of the household. This aspect of the layout accords very well with conclusions that have been drawn on the basis of Athenian texts, which imply that such surveillance within the household was an important mechanism through which moral codes were enforced and reinforced (for example Hunter 1994).

The transition from the relatively small, open house-types of the Early Iron Age to the larger, subdivided dwellings of the Classical period also implies a radical change which affected not only the organisation of day-to-day domestic activity, but also the way in which the domestic sphere as a whole was conceptualised. Creation of a variety of rooms during the later period suggests a desire to provide areas which could be used to separate different activities, and the individuals carrying them out, at any one time. The appearance of a specialised andron in some houses seems to be part of this development and offers an insight into the kind of social dynamics which may have been operating (in this case probably requiring separation of individuals on the basis of sex and household membership). The emergence of this more segmented type of house therefore seems to indicate a new set of expectations about what constituted correct patterns of behaviour in the domestic sphere. A context for these changes is provided by the increasing stress being placed on inheritance as a criterion for membership of the citizen body during the fifth century at Athens and perhaps also in other cities. Constructing a house which was segmented in this way would have facilitated the separation of the women of the household from male outsiders, and in turn enhanced claims by the male householder that he was indeed the father of his wife's children. A man's house thus seems to have become an important symbol by this period, not only demonstrating the general prosperity of the household as a whole through its size and decoration, but also embodying his conformity to a particular set of social rules through the organisation of interior space.

On present evidence, then, the kind of isolated environment which is generally assumed to have been an integral part of sympotic practice would not have been found widely in domestic contexts until the sixth or fifth century, and the majority of the examples currently known date to the late fifth century or later. It therefore seems likely that our image of an event taking place in an enclosed space in a private house also belongs – like the texts from which it is derived – specifically to the fifth and also the fourth century. The creation of the andron thus forms part of a broader trend taking place during this period towards the physical separation of different individuals and activities in households. In fact, even during the fifth and fourth centuries not all houses included a decorated andron of the type discussed above. At Olynthus, for example, only a minority of the fifty-three fully excavated houses have identifiable andrones.

At other sites the numbers of excavated properties are much smaller and it is more difficult to get an overview, but it does seem that scholars have been keen to identify rooms as andrones even where evidence in support of their identifications is limited or lacking. In some cases this might simply be because some of the key features such as the location of the doorway or traces of wall and floor decoration are no longer preserved.

In others the architecture of the room and layout of the house makes it questionable whether a symposium, narrowly defined, could have been held there. For example, in a rural farm house at Vari in Attica, which dates to the second half of the fourth century BCE, the excavators identified as a potential setting for the symposium a space (rooms III and IV) which had a bench on one wall, although, as they comment, the foundation for a hearth would have hampered the placement of other couches, and there were none of the other distinguishing features such as a square shape, an off-centre doorway or wall and floor decoration (Jones *et al.* 1973, 434–435). Even if it were used for drinking parties, the elongated shape and awkwardness for placement of furniture would have produced a different atmosphere and social dynamic from the enclosed square rooms of this type seen elsewhere. There is a similar lack of correspondence with many of the classic andron features in rooms identified as domestic androngs at a variety of other sites. In at least some instances it seems likely that scholars have assumed that an andron was present in every house and have assigned that name to the most plausible-looking room. In other cases some features are present, for example a square shape and off-centre doorway, while others, such as architectural decoration, are lacking. Houses in rural locations – either in villages or deme centres, or isolated farmsteads – seem to have had androngs more rarely, while those in larger, urban, settlements are provided with them more frequently, although, as the example of Olynthus shows, even in a large settlement such a room cannot be identified in every house.

To sum up, the classic form of andron visible in houses of the later fifth and fourth centuries is not a feature of every house of this date, and it cannot readily be traced back into the Archaic period either on the basis of architectural evidence or through a distinctive patterning of finds of pottery associated with drinking. But if clear examples of a specialised andron can only be found in excavated houses at such a relatively late date, what are the implications for the social context of wine consumption before this time? Should we assume that drinking parties took place only in the civic and religious spheres and not in private houses? Or should we be looking for a more flexible or alternative model for wine consumption to the traditional symposium model? To explore these questions, I want to introduce an additional form of evidence, namely drinking scenes from painted pottery. These images obviously constitute selective representations which include myth and fantasy as well as elements of the painters' contemporary world, and they play on the experience and expectations of an acculturated audience in different ways. We should therefore be wary of interpreting them as literal 'snapshots' of 'real-life' occasions. At the same time, however, they must have been comprehensible to ancient viewers, and so they are likely to incorporate familiar elements and can be used to suggest a range of possible scenarios for domestic wine consumption.

IMAGES OF SOCIAL DRINKING IN ARCHAIC AND CLASSICAL GREECE

Although images on painted pottery have often appeared in discussions of the symposium, they have frequently tended to be approached with the aim of supporting or illustrating the literary-based model of sympotic behaviour, rather than as sources of information which can be investigated in their own right. Their use has frequently also been limited to anecdotal references to one or two vessels, rather than extending to examinations of larger samples of vessels which might offer a more representative picture.[4] But an overview of a substantial group of such vessels, paying attention to ways in which the images they carry change through time, shows that there was significant change in the details represented.[5] Scenes which depict reclining drinkers are generally taken to represent symposia, and many incorporate a variety of the features regarded as central to the definition of the symposium: the participants recline and although their architectural surroundings are not normally shown in detail, elements of the furnishings are often included such as couches, tables and footstools. Representations of a variety of cups and larger pottery vessels tend to feature prominently. In addition participants are shown engaged in a range of other pursuits: playing music and/or singing, games such as kottabos (flicking wine from a cup at a target) and sexual activity with male and/or female partners (the latter customarily interpreted as entertainers or prostitutes). In some instances these scenes are clearly mythological, featuring gods and/or heroes who are identifiable either indirectly by their various attributes or directly through name labels. In others, name labels apparently refer to members of contemporary society. In the majority of cases, though, the figures are

---

[4] There are a few exceptions, notably Schmitt-Pantel 1990a.

[5] My discussion here is based on a sample of 57,840 vessels recorded as part of the on-line version of Oxford University's Beazley archive of Attic pottery. The vessels are dated to fifty-year periods which progress at twenty-five-year intervals. This means that short-term change becomes somewhat blurred because the periods covered appear to overlap. The vessels themselves are not double-counted, however, and the system has the advantage of effectively minimising potential problems caused by uncertainties in the precise dating sequences. This level of chronological resolution still enables comparison between changes taking place in the ceramic iconography and those taking place in the architecture and organisation of the houses themselves.

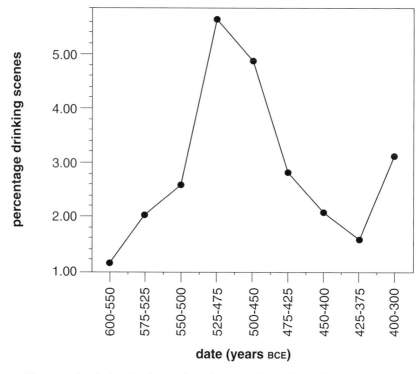

Figure 3.4 Graph showing change through time in the numbers of scenes depicting drinking as a percentage of total scenes

nameless and apparently generic. Such scenes were created throughout the period from about 600 to 300 BCE. They are most common around 500 BCE, after which time they slowly decline in numbers (Figure 3.4), although at any one time they represent only a relatively small percentage of the total number of scenes on painted pottery.

The iconography of these images is difficult to interpret and there are also changes through time in the details represented. While it is possible that these are simply a result of changing artistic conventions, the patterns are internally consistent and offer a basis for comparison with the domestic architecture. It is often implied or assumed that at least some of these drinking scenes show domestic interiors, but upon close examination the images themselves suggest the possibility of a variety of underlying types of social occasion which may have taken place in different settings. On the earlier vessels food is commonly shown, although this element declines rapidly in popularity and has almost disappeared by the mid fifth

Plate 3.2 Attic red-figure kylix depicting social drinking with columns in the background. (Attributed to the Brygos painter, *c.* 490–480 BCE. British Museum inventory number E68: copyright Trustees of the British Museum.)

century BCE. This is important, since if the traditional narrow definition of symposium is meaningful, it seems likely that at least some of these earlier scenes do not show a symposium in the strict sense, but instead represent a deipnon or meal, which might have preceded a symposium. Alternatively, as Pauline Schmitt-Pantel argues, such scenes may represent some other occasion entirely, perhaps one which is civic or religious, rather than domestic in character (Schmitt-Pantel 1990a). Where an architectural setting or background is shown this, too, sometimes calls into question the identification of a domestic symposium.

A notable element of a few examples is the incorporation of columns into the background (Plate 3.2). There is a steady rise in the number of such scenes from their first appearance during the second half of the sixth century, through to a peak in the second half of the fifth century BCE. The presence of columns implies a setting where roof supports are necessary and may indicate a large civic or religious building. If the context is to be understood as domestic, columns would indicate a semi-outdoor location, namely the courtyard and portico. The inclusion of tendrils of ivy or vines,

Plate 3.3 Attic red-figure kylix showing drinkers apparently reclining on the floor.
(Attributed to the Ashby Painter, *c.* 500 BCE. British Museum inventory number E64:
copyright Trustees of the British Museum.)

which appear in some of these images, may be symbolic of the consumption of wine and its association with Dionysus, but may perhaps sometimes have been intended more literally as an evocation of such an outdoor setting. Some of these scenes clearly show couches on which the participants recline, but others show the drinkers only with cushions beneath them (Plate 3.3). It may be that the artist has sometimes chosen to omit the couches in order to focus attention on the participants themselves, but there are images in which the drinkers seem to be intended to be understood as reclining on cushions set directly on the floor, since standing figures and vessels are included on the same ground line. A lack of couches may therefore be important, because it might imply relatively informal surroundings which could be adapted for reclining and then changed for some other purpose simply by removal or rearrangement of the cushions.

Taken together, it seems possible that some of the occasions depicted, particularly those of fifth-century date where columns are more frequent and couches shown less often, did not take place in a formal andron at all but instead were located in multi-functional spaces which could be adapted for the purpose by moving couches or cushions around. It is possible to suggest several potential domestic locations which need not necessarily be mutually exclusive. One possibility is suggested both by iconographic and by textual evidence, and that is that such events may sometimes have taken place in domestic porticos or courtyards.

We know, from looking at the distribution of artefacts in fifth- and fourth-century houses, that domestic space was used flexibly, with activities relocated to different areas of the house in order to accommodate changing circumstances such as seasonal variation in temperature. The wide variety of items found in courtyards suggests that these areas, in particular, were used for a range of different activities (Nevett 1999, 36–39). It would have been relatively easy, and quite consistent with this pattern, for couches or cushions to be moved outside into the courtyard, and in fact precisely this is also attested in literature, for example in Plato's *Protagoras* 315C. The use of the courtyard in this way would explain the appearance of columns in some images, but would also have given the social occasion in question a rather different atmosphere from that usually envisaged for the symposium. A courtyard location would have retained some privacy from outsiders because courtyards were relatively enclosed. Nevertheless, the party could have been observed closely by other members of the household who were not participating, for example respectable female members of household occupying the interior rooms. We can only speculate on the possible effect of this on the event itself, but it may not have created quite the atmosphere of separation from normality which is often envisaged for the symposium, and so behaviour may perhaps have been more restrained.

CONCLUSIONS: SITUATING GREEK DOMESTIC SYMPOSIA

The evidence explored in this chapter suggests that the symposium as narrowly defined in the Introduction is likely to have been just one of a variety of types of occasion at which wine was consumed in the domestic sphere. Both the flexible way in which space was used in Greek houses, and some of the iconography associated with drinking, indicate that, even in houses which seem to lack a formal andron, wine consumption may well have taken place in a less formal setting, in a courtyard or in a multi-purpose room which was adapted through the use of portable furnishings such as couches and cushions. This should perhaps lead scholars to reconsider how rigidly the term symposium is defined, and to revisit the implications of its use and the frequency with which it is applied in different contexts. Such conclusions also have more far-reaching consequences. For example, the kind of sexually explicit and otherwise transgressive activities which are thought to have required physical isolation from the remainder of the household may not have been an element of drinking in more open settings, or they may have been considered less threatening to social order than has sometimes been assumed. At the same time there are implications for our understanding of the wider cultural and historical context during the Archaic period, and, in particular, customary assumptions about the performance context for the lyric poetry associated with this time. Again, without the kind of enclosed, separate space within the household which is often envisaged, such performances are perhaps more plausibly located in a non-domestic space such as a sanctuary. Such a location makes sense in the context of recent suggestions that during the early first millennium BCE cult activity originated in the houses of community leaders and that religious functions were gradually moved to separate sacred buildings (early temples). Drinking parties may perhaps have followed this route too, initially forming part of the religious sphere, with more formalised drinking parties in the private context coming as a later development.

The fact that the canonical, enclosed, andron with off-centre doorway and marked spaces for couches appeared at a relatively late date also has important implications. Its creation is linked with a wider and more dramatic change in the practical and symbolic role played by the private house as a whole: with a radical increase in overall size and number of rooms, the domestic sphere came increasingly to constitute not only a place to live but also a tool through which to project support for the values associated with citizenship (compare Nevett 2009a). Housing therefore offered a means of asserting membership of the citizen body itself. Alongside the privacy and social control afforded by this new house-form, the frequency with which an andron was included among the more specialised rooms at sites like Olynthus – and the fact that its presence was sometimes signalled on the exterior of the house – suggest that, in some communities at least, the symposium had by this time become an important and widespread symbol of citizenship (compare Schmitt-Pantel and Tchernia 2004, 44). Rather than a preserve of the elite, the symposium therefore seems to have been viewed as an activity in which most or all citizens might participate. Nevertheless, the location of the andron amongst the domestic quarters might also imply that its use for the symposium was relatively rare compared with other uses which may have been made of the room, and that, for some people at least, the idea of participation in the symposium – embodied in the possession of the andron itself – may have been more important than the reality of actually holding symposia with any frequency.

CHAPTER 4

Housing and cultural identity: Delos, between Greece and Rome

Cleopatra, daughter of Adrastus of Myrrhinous, set up this image
of her husband Dioscorides, son of Theodorus of Myrrhinous, who
dedicated the two Delphic tripods of silver by each doorpost in the
temple of Apollo, in the archonship of Timarchus at Athens.

Inscriptions de Délos 1987, inscribed on a statue-base in
House III.I, Theatre Quarter, Delos, 138/137 BCE[1]

All societies have culturally acceptable uses of domestic space.

Pader 1997, 72

INTRODUCTION

In or about the year 138/137 BCE, on the island of Delos, the sculpted
portraits of a woman and a man were set up inside a house in an old
residential neighbourhood of the main town (Plate 4.1). The figures are
made of white marble and are depicted at life-size. Now missing their
heads, each one poses in a manner comparable with other images of this
period. He has his right arm crooked under the folds of a himation or
robe – a stance used in Greek civic and funerary sculpture since the fourth
century BCE. She is pulling tight a thin shawl to reveal the folds of a thicker
dress beneath, in a manner popular in sculpted figures of women from the
third and second centuries BCE. An inscription on the statue-base, written
in Greek, identifies the couple and is quoted above. It refers to a gift made
to the famous temple of the god Apollo on Delos, by Dioscorides, son
of Theodorus, who came from the community of Myrrhinous (modern
Merenda) in the territory of Athens.

The house in which this pair of statues was displayed is generally assumed
to have belonged at one time to the couple depicted. It is fairly typical of

[1] Timarchus is known to have been archon (annual magistrate) for a year beginning in 138 and finishing
in 137 BCE. It is unclear whether the date refers to the setting up of the portraits or to the donation
of the silver tripods to the temple of Apollo.

Plate 4.1 Replica of the monument to Cleopatra and Dioscorides *in situ*

the larger homes in this district of the town, known by archaeologists as
the Theatre Quarter. The plot the house occupies (Theatre Quarter House
III.1) is irregular, a feature which probably results from the extension of
what was originally a small courtyard house which may go back as early as
the third century BCE. By the time of Cleopatra and Dioscorides there were
twelve rooms arranged around two open courtyards (Figure 4.1). At the
time the house was expanded, or shortly afterwards, the eastern courtyard
was converted into a decorated peristyle and it was here that Cleopatra's
monument was located. During one phase of renovations, probably in
conjunction with the installation of the monument itself, a doorway to a
room lying on the north side of the courtyard (room F) was blocked. The
threshold was left in position and formed a foundation on which the base
of the monument was placed. It seems likely that the entrance to room F
was deliberately moved so that the statues could be set up there instead
(Kreeb 1985b, 21). But what was so special about this particular location?
Why was the statue group put here, inside a private house, rather than,
as was the usual custom at this time, in a public place where it would
have been seen by more people? Consideration of the architectural context
for the monument (Plate 4.1) suggests that the images of Cleopatra and
her husband were positioned in order to be visible clearly from the house

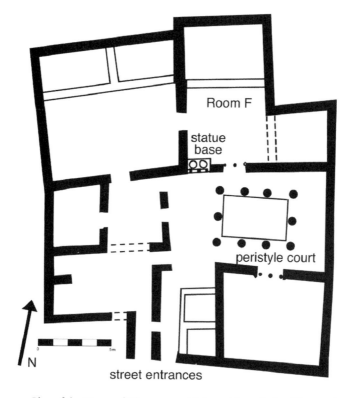

Figure 4.1 Plan of the House of Cleopatra and Dioscorides at Delos (Theatre Quarter House III.1)

entrance and, if the door was open, from the street beyond. In fact the narrow alley down which the entrance to the house lies seems to channel the eye of the viewer through the doorway towards the figures. The overall visual effect would have been enhanced by the fact that they stood within a niche, framed by the former doorway.

This concern with the visual impact of the house's interior on a viewer standing at the entrance parallels an arrangement seen at a later date in the large atrium houses of Roman Campania (discussed below in Chapter 5). But the formal symmetry and axiality in the arrangement of rooms seen in Campania is not found in this case. Here, the columns of the interior peristyle could only have been glimpsed obliquely on the viewer's right, and the focal point is clearly the statue group itself rather than the architecture of the interior space or the inhabitants set within that space. In drawing attention to the inside of the house from its entrance, this building also creates a different impression from Greek houses of the Classical period (discussed in Chapter 3), which tend to form enclosed environments featuring screen walls and angled corridors designed to shut out the world of the street. Nevertheless, if we look more closely at the plan of the house in which Cleopatra and Dioscorides' images stood, we can see that in reality the viewer's gaze could not have penetrated very far: parts of the house which would have seen a lot of activity, namely the majority of the peristyle together with a second court to the west and the entrances to the surrounding rooms, are all out of view. Even with the door open, the inhabitants would have been visible from the street only when moving between the house's eastern and western sections. Furthermore, a second entrance to the house, immediately to the west and opening into what was probably a service area, provided an alternative means of entering and leaving the house without offering even this glimpse of the main living accommodation in the interior.

The organisation of Cleopatra and Dioscorides' house and the location of the monument within raise a number of questions about the inhabitants of Delos towards the close of the first millennium BCE. To what extent was this apparent desire to invite the viewer's gaze into the house a widespread characteristic of households in the town? What might such an eye-catching arrangement indicate about the way the occupants of this and any similar houses related to their neighbours and to the town at large? And what might the mode or modes of conceiving domestic space have to tell us about Delian society at this time? In order to address these questions we first need to situate the house within its immediate physical, historical and cultural context.

The island of Delos was occupied from at least the Late Bronze Age, and during the Archaic and Classical periods it was known throughout Greece and beyond for its sanctuary of Apollo. Excavation has revealed extensive remains of that sanctuary and of many streets and house-blocks in the town which surrounded it, so that it is possible to study the layout of about one hundred different houses. Most of these were part of larger blocks or insulae in which separate properties shared party walls. Individual house-plots are frequently irregularly shaped, and the different dwellings are often accessed from narrow, winding streets. This pattern is most evident in the Theatre Quarter, where a number of residential blocks have been excavated in their entirety (Figure 4.2). Some properties were probably occupied for a century or more, and most were modified and rebuilt over time, making it difficult to know exactly when they were first constructed or what they looked like in their earliest forms. Many of the smaller ones may originally

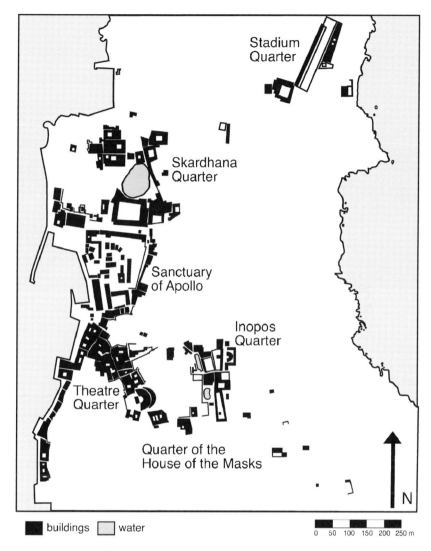

Figure 4.2 Plan of Delos town showing the locations of the different housing quarters

have followed a standardised layout, with the main rooms accessed from an open court via a shallow anteroom, colonnade or pastas.

Compared with most Greek houses of earlier periods the standard of preservation of the Delian structures is very good, owing to the relatively large amount of stone used in construction and the absence of significant

Plate 4.2 Interior of the House of the Hill at Delos, showing the preserved height of the
walls and the locations of windows onto the court

later building activity on the island. The walls of the lower storeys normally
stand to a height of at least a metre, and the locations of doorways, and
sometimes also window openings, are clear (Plate 4.2). In some instances
a plaster coating survived on wall surfaces at the time of excavation, and
this sometimes showed traces of decoration. On interior walls a range of
different treatments have been found, from simple coloured plaster panels
and dados through to the elaborate so-called Masonry Style decoration in
which moulded plaster imitated stone architectural elements, picked out in
different colours. Figured friezes are particularly characteristic (Bruno 1985,
3). The evidence from exterior walls is less extensive, but here, too, plaster
was used. In some instances it provided a base for 'liturgical paintings',
which were images in vernacular style with religious associations, often
located close to altars beside house entrances and, to judge by the numerous layers of successive overpainting, intended for temporary display only
(Bezerra de Meneses and Sarian 1973, with previous references). Today, the
plaster on both exterior and interior walls has frequently deteriorated or
even disappeared completely since excavation, owing to the effects of wind
and rain. Interior floors in the Delos houses were often cobbled, tiled or
made of mortar or mosaic. Tessellated mosaics (composed of small tesserae

or cubes) followed a variety of forms. Some were plain white or white with a scattering of dark cubes. Others incorporated geometric borders and patterns, sometimes even including elaborate polychrome panels or emblemata (figurative panels), which featured representations of objects or figured scenes.

Substantial changes to the decoration, layout, and even the boundaries of house-plots, can be seen in walled-up doors or traced through differences in the flooring materials used in a single room. It therefore seems that the occupants readily adapted the architecture to suit changing tastes and requirements. As in the House of Cleopatra and Dioscorides, many alterations were aimed at enlarging existing houses and installing additional decorative features such as colonnaded peristyle courts. We can view the form and decoration of the houses during their final phase of occupation as resulting from a combination of decisions taken over a number of generations concerning what to build, how to decorate, what to modify and what to leave in place. (For example, assuming that Cleopatra and Dioscorides' monument stands in its original location, their images must have been retained *in situ* by several succeeding generations of occupants, from their installation in the late second century BCE until the destruction of the house sometime in the first century BCE.)

In Cleopatra and Dioscorides' lifetime Delos was what we might call today a 'multi-cultural' community. Its location and history linked it with the cities of the Greek world, especially Athens, which had political control during the Classical period. In 166 BCE the Romans returned Delos to Athenian hands after a relatively short period of independence. The community flourished and the population expanded rapidly under this second Athenian domination: Delos became one of the largest commercial ports in the Mediterranean, serving as a centre for the exchange of a variety of goods including slaves. As some of the large numbers of inscriptions found here show, much of that trade was dominated by merchants from communities in Italy including Campania, but they also provide evidence for the presence of traders from as far away as the Levantine coast – modern Syria and Lebanon. Monika Trümper has suggested that some of the changes made to the layout and decoration of houses at this time might have been linked with this influx of foreign merchants (Trümper 1998, 132). Delos' prosperity was only short-lived, however: during the first century BCE at least two attacks from the sea (in 88 and 69 BCE) seem to have led to the destruction and widespread abandonment of most of the settlement, including the houses, over a relatively brief period. Although the Delian landscape was subsequently farmed by the inhabitants of nearby islands, it was never substantially reoccupied, so that the archaeological remains are relatively well preserved.

The combination of different cultural influences on the island makes Delos an ideal context for studying the effects on individual households of the complex process of acculturation which took place as Rome's territory expanded geographically outwards and its people came into contact with individuals from neighbouring societies. It is this issue which is the central question to be explored in this chapter. In the past scholars viewed Rome's relationship with other cultures from a colonialist perspective, interpreting the expansion of Roman power as also involving cultural 'Romanisation'. More recently, however, the adoption of post-colonial ideas has highlighted the fact that Rome itself encompassed a plurality of differentiated local Italian groups, each with its own language and culture, and that the process of interaction between these and the populations out of whose lands the Empire was ultimately created was multi-layered, with influences passing in all directions. It has been suggested that as a result of this interaction a variety of distinctive new local cultures were formed. Studies of different geographical regions have shown increasingly that it is impossible to generalise about how such relationships worked; instead, it is necessary to examine specific areas and cultures individually in order to understand these processes in their own contexts.

The evidence from Delos provides an opportunity to investigate ways in which cultural interaction may have affected one specific community, and in particular to test in detail some of the general models for this process. These include the idea that, rather than the obliteration or transformation of earlier local customs, contact resulted in the creation of new and distinctive 'hybrid' cultures which had elements of, but were independent from, those of the individual populations who were interacting with each other. Delos is an especially interesting context in which to explore the validity of this idea and to ask how such a process may have worked in practice, since the island came under Roman influence at an early date, prior to the creation of the Principate in 27 BCE, a time when Roman culture itself was relatively fluid. The excavated houses are also a particularly revealing source because they vary considerably in size and in the quantity of decoration, suggesting that they were inhabited by families varying in their wealth and status. It is therefore possible to explore how cultural interaction affected households at different socio-economic levels, in contrast with many studies of the expansion of Rome which have tended to focus on acculturation only at an elite level.

Before looking more closely at the evidence, one analytical problem which needs to be tackled is that culture itself is a difficult concept to define, either in an ancient or even in a modern context. Archaeologically it has been common to use similarities in styles of architecture and/or artefacts in order to identify and to differentiate between cultures, but such a technique is of limited utility in relation to the Roman world, where individual styles are very widespread (Terrenato 1999, 25) and where the significance of different stylistic types may have depended on aspects of their context and usage which may be invisible to a modern observer (James 2001, 203–204).[2] In the towns and cities of the modern world we are used to seeing people from a range of geographical and ethnic backgrounds living and working in a single location. At the same time differentiated communities often emerge, expressing their cultural affiliations in a variety of ways including through their language, dress, cuisine and architecture. Sociologist Stuart Hall has recently emphasised the roles played by individuals in consciously establishing their own cultural identities and has stressed the fact that this is a continual process of negotiation, of establishing boundaries, of masking differences and of articulating similarities, a process for which he uses the psychoanalytical term 'identification', in preference to 'identity' (Hall 1996, 2–4). Hall sees identification as a concept which is particularly relevant to the modern world, and he connects it with the phenomenon of globalisation. Nevertheless, the features he picks out as characteristic, such as the use of a concept of the 'Other' and difference as a means of self-definition, are ideas which have already been shown to be fundamental in Classical Antiquity, particularly in the Greek world (for example Cartledge 2002, *passim*). The concept of identification offers a useful tool for studying cultural interaction in the ancient world. Its stress on the active role taken by individuals brings a new perspective to the discussion of cultural contact and a human scale which is particularly suited to analysis through archaeological evidence. At the same time the stress it places on shifting definitions emphasises the complexity of the models needed in order to interpret the archaeological material.

---

[2] In the context of Delos artistic styles and influences themselves are also difficult measures to use since, although a variety of themes occur which might be linked with different cultural traditions, the artistic techniques themselves are Greek (Bruno 1985, 13–14), so the symbolic significance of individual motifs is unclear, and may indeed have changed during the time over which decorative elements were in use. Some of the possibilities opened up by using the iconography of individual decorative elements from a different domestic context (a house in Roman Carthage) are, however, explored in detail in Chapter 6.

For an analysis of Delian housing, the potential individual agency high-lighted by the identification process means that attempting to work out the geographical origins and backgrounds of specific households would be simplistic, since it would underestimate the power of the inhabitants to play different roles in different contexts, actively constructing their own identities. At a more pragmatic level, most houses must have been inhab-ited over a number of generations, and it is normally impossible to associate a specific occupation phase with any single individual or household (see Nevett, forthcoming); Cleopatra and Dioscorides' house is unusual in this regard. The goal of this chapter is therefore to take a collective, rather than individual, view of the process of identification, exploring patterns of acculturation within the community as a whole. In particular I shall focus on the interface between the interior world of the household and the exte-rior world of the community as a whole, asking whether there is evidence of multiple conceptions of the relationship between the two which might suggest underlying differences in the cultural norms governing domestic social behaviour. I address this question by exploring whether the House of Cleopatra and Dioscorides is typical in the extent to which visual access from the street to the interior is permitted and by suggesting how Delian patterns of visual access may relate to those seen in Greek and Roman housing more generally.

THE HOUSE OF CLEOPATRA AND DIOSCORIDES IN CONTEXT: THE DECORATION, ARCHITECTURE AND LAYOUT OF OTHER DELIAN HOUSES

Cleopatra and Dioscorides' images are unusual both in their subject mat-ter and their location. A few other examples of portrait sculpture have been found in domestic contexts on the island. More commonly, however, the subjects of domestic sculptures at the site are mythological. Similarly, in most cases where we know the exact locations in which sculptures were dis-played in domestic contexts, they were not readily visible from the street.[3] Out of eleven other examples, only in one case could an image have been seen through an open street door: in House IIIS in the Theatre Quarter,

[3] Unfortunately, although a substantial number of statues and fragments have been found in domestic contexts at the site, in most cases we do not know precisely where in the house they were displayed, either because no base was found *in situ*, or because the information which would have revealed the original locations of the individual pieces was not recorded at the time of excavation (Kreeb 1985a, 47–51).

a life-size marble Artemis with a deer would have been visible in a niche on the opposite side of the courtyard (Kreeb 1985a, 34–35). In two other properties a visitor penetrating the vestibule or entrance corridor to stand on the edge of the courtyard would have been able to look across at a large sculptural group. In the House of the Herms (in the Inopos Quarter) the base for a statue group is preserved on the back wall of one of the main downstairs rooms, where it would have been seen across the peristyle by anyone using the upper entrance (Kreeb 1985a, 38–40). In the Lake House (Skardhana Quarter) a female statue stood in a niche which would, again, have been visible across the courtyard (Kreeb 1985a, 40–41).

These latter examples suggest the possibility that Cleopatra and Dioscorides' monument may have been designed to make an impact on a visitor who had already entered the house and that its visibility from the street may be coincidental. This is an important distinction which could potentially tell us much about the nature of Delian society. If the monument was aimed at people coming into the house, then it can be regarded as a continuation of a Greek tradition of decorating the areas most likely to be seen by visitors, which goes back to at least the fifth century BCE. If, however, the aim was to catch the eye of passers-by outside, this would represent a departure from that tradition in that, while decoration of house exteriors may have been used as a way of attracting attention or as a medium for competitive display between neighbours (compare Nevett 2009b), the interiors were normally hidden.

It is not possible to decide which of the two alternative interpretations is more plausible based on our surviving information about Delian domestic sculpture alone: there are simply too few houses where we can be sure about the way in which the sculpture was displayed. Nevertheless, we can explore whether creating a view from the street itself was important by looking for other decorative features, and assessing whether these were designed to be seen from the street through open doors. This can be done based on the plans of eighty-nine completely excavated houses whose pattern of organisation can be reconstructed relatively well. Although these represent only a fraction of the original number of houses in the town, they do provide a cross-section of structures of different sizes and from different neighbourhoods, including from around Cleopatra and Dioscorides' house in the Theatre Quarter, from the Inopos Quarter and from the Quarter of the House of the Masks. The newer Stadium and Skardhana Quarters are also represented (see Figure 4.2). The overall impression is one of diversity in size and layout.

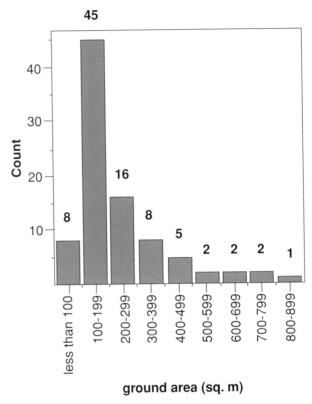

Figure 4.3 Graph showing the range in ground area of the Delian houses analysed here

In terms of size, this sample covers a wide range, from a ground area of 53 up to 866 square metres (Figure 4.3). However, the majority are at the lower end of this scale, with a mean house size of 228 square metres, and in fact 53 per cent fall in the range between 100 and 200 square metres. (For comparison, a two-bedroom apartment in modern Athens might cover an area of around 70 to 100 square metres.) A further eight houses (10 per cent) are smaller than 100 square metres, while the remaining 37 per cent cover a wide range from 200 to over 800 square metres. Such variety suggests that these properties were occupied by households of different economic and social statuses. The number of spaces (rooms, corridors and courtyards combined) in each house also varies considerably, ranging between only two and a total of fifteen, although the majority of properties (52 per cent) had

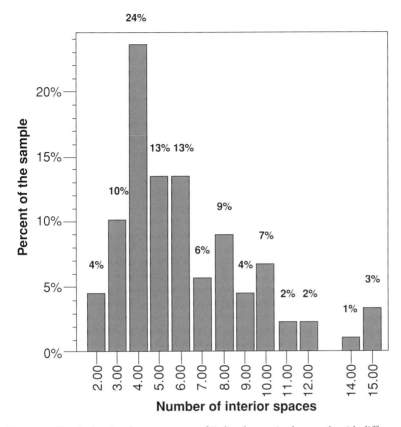

Figure 4.4 Graph showing the percentages of Delian houses in the sample with different numbers of spaces

between three and six spaces each (Figure 4.4). While among the smaller houses there is a close relationship between the number of spaces and the ground area the structure covers, among those with six or more rooms this is not the case: a calculation of the mean ground area occupied by houses with different numbers of rooms shows that the standard deviation (the amount of variation around the mean) is much higher for these buildings, indicating that while some large houses were divided into numerous small rooms, others had fewer, larger, ones (Figure 4.5). A relationship does exist between the size of a house and the design of its interior courtyard, with courts in smaller houses tending to lack any form of portico or to make use of an anteroom or pastas arrangement, while the larger houses normally have a colonnaded peristyle (Figure 4.6). There are, however, a few larger

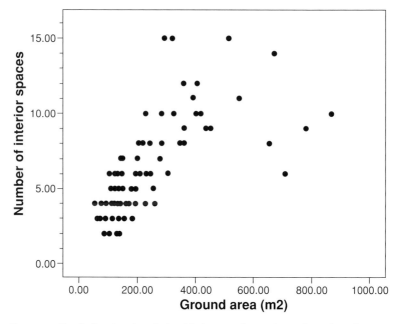

Figure 4.5 Graph showing the relationship between house size and number of interior spaces in the Delian sample

houses which retain the simpler forms of courtyard, so that size was not the only factor in determining which form was selected.

CULTURAL INFLUENCES ON DELIAN HOUSE LAYOUT

When viewed in the context of this wider group of houses, the location and prominence of Cleopatra and Dioscorides' monument can be interpreted as combining two different attitudes towards the opening up of the domestic interior to the street outside, each of which is visible in other houses from the town. At one end of the spectrum, in a small number of cases the angle of the main entrance means that, even with the door open, the interior would have been completely screened from view from the street. In most cases, though (seventy-six out of the seventy-nine in which the location and form of the entrance could be determined), it would have been possible to see into either a vestibule or a courtyard. In many (forty-seven houses or 62 per cent of those) it would have been possible to see further, into another space beyond. In a few (eleven examples) the alignment of doorways would

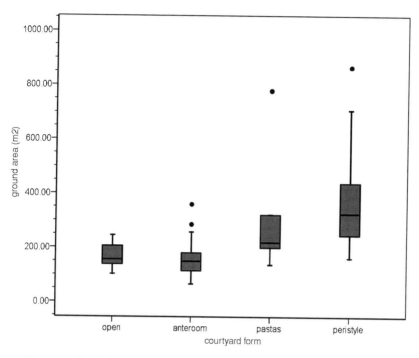

Figure 4.6 Graph showing the relationship between house size and courtyard-type at Delos

have meant that another one or two spaces were visible. To what extent might doors have been left open deliberately to reveal these interior views?

One way to address this question is by trying to assess whether the interior was arranged so that decorative elements were visible from the street, or whether they were more often hidden until a visitor actually entered the house. Aside from the sculpture, which was discussed earlier, there are a variety of potentially decorative features surviving in areas visible from the street entrance. Particularly noticeable are mosaic emblemata and peristyle courts. In houses possessing either of these features (a total of forty-five houses) their presence was normally clear to visitors. (89 per cent of peristyles were visible either from the street door or from the entrance corridor or vestibule, and in 90 per cent of houses with mosaic emblemata, at least one was visible from the same locations.) The distribution of each feature is slightly different, however. In the majority of houses featuring mosaic emblemata, examples came into view only once a visitor had crossed the vestibule, suggesting that they were aimed specifically at visitors. In contrast, the peristyle could in many cases have been seen from outside in the street, suggesting that passers-by may have been expected to glimpse them from the exterior. Three peristyle houses in the sample lack any form of vestibule or entrance corridor. In many of the others, although the street entrance does not open directly into the peristyle, it seems that there was generally no attempt to screen the peristyle from view, suggesting that it was felt to be acceptable for the peristyle to be viewable from the street, and that indeed it may deliberately have been placed on display to be seen by passers-by.

Three specific houses offer the most striking evidence that this effect was probably intentional: in the Diadumenos House (Skardhana Quarter), the House of the Dolphins (Quarter of the House of the Masks) and the House of the Trident (Theatre Quarter) the corridor, peristyle and the façade of the main living rooms beyond are all aligned, and each house presents a symmetrical vista which is enhanced with mosaic emblemata and painted decoration (Figure 4.7). In these cases there definitely seems to be an element of self-presentation to passers-by in the street as well as to guests entering the vestibule. This arrangement would have meant that, when the street doors were left open, activity in the centre of the peristyle would have been visible from the street, although the relatively long, narrow entrance corridor (a in Figure 4.7) in each case would have restricted visual access to the spaces on both sides which led to the living quarters. In all three houses a side entrance leads into the peristyle at right-angles to the major visual axis, providing an alternative point of entry into the house.

Although these three houses represent only a small fraction of the examples analysed here, they are significant in demonstrating that some of the occupants of Delos town did have an awareness of, and a desire to use, some of the same principles governing the organisation and layout of the houses that are seen in the later houses in Campania, and which seem to represent part of a longer Italian housing tradition. These principles include the use of monumentality and axiality, and the possibilities offered by the domestic sphere as a formalised setting which the householder could manipulate as a backdrop to enhance his personal status, creating an impression of his own wealth and power.[4] (The actual organisation of space is, of course, somewhat different from the Campanian houses, most noticeably in that the Delian houses without exception lack an interior hall or 'atrium'.)

---

[4] For the shift towards monumentality in house construction in Etruscan contexts see, for example Izzet 2001. Her Figure 2 demonstrates early axiality in house planning although she does not specifically comment on this.

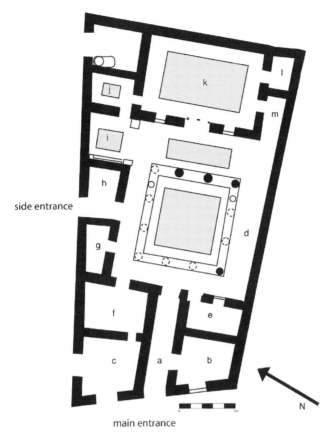

side entrance

main entrance

Figure 4.7 Plan of the House of the Trident at Delos (Theatre Quarter House II A)

Alongside this visual openness of the interior of the house to the gaze of outsiders, there also seems to have been a physical openness in some houses which facilitated movement between the interior and exterior. While seventy-two of the houses (81 per cent) have only a single street-entrance, a significant minority, like the three symmetrically organised houses discussed above, have two (fourteen houses or 16 per cent), and a couple of houses have three.[5] Viewed from a practical perspective, multiple entrances might have been particularly useful in large houses, enabling specific rooms such as stores and food preparation areas, or reception rooms for entertaining guests, to be accessed easily. In practice, though, the situation is

---

[5] These figures exclude entrances to rooms unconnected with the main part of the house.

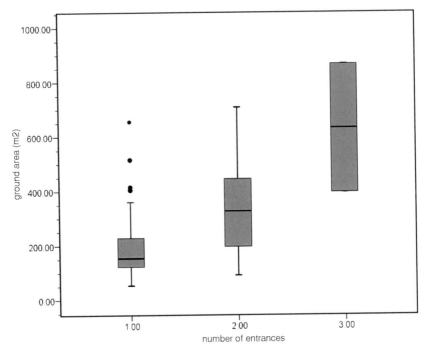

Figure 4.8 Graph showing the relationship between house-area and number of entrances
in the Delian sample

more complex. In many cases both entrances ultimately gave into the same
space, the central court. At the same time, the relationship with house size
is not straightforward: there are some small houses with two entrances,
while some of the largest have only one (Figure 4.8).

Therefore, although in the houses with more than one entrance the
choice of which of them to use may to some extent have been function-
ally determined, there were probably also social and cultural distinctions
determining which entrance was used on which occasion. For instance,
in the House of the Trident the main central entrance is enhanced with
marble architectural mouldings. These, along with its impressive vista, may
indicate a formal entrance aimed at outsiders entering as guests. The side
entrance in the same house, which also gave access to the upper storey,
is narrower and more plainly decorated and may perhaps have been used
on a day-to-day basis as well as by occupants of an upstairs apartment. In
this and the other two axially planned houses the second entrance would
have made it possible to enter or leave the house without opening the main

door and thereby involuntarily exposing to outside view anyone using the large living room (commonly known as the oecus), which is the visual focus of that entrance and faces it directly across the court (Figure 4.7, room k). Alternatively, if the main door were intentionally left open, that same visual axis could have been used as a way of framing the occupants of the oecus, creating an impressive aspect for passers-by in the street or for visitors entering by that route.

In short, therefore, compared with the Greek houses of earlier periods, those on Delos were often relatively permeable to the outside gaze. The few cases where a symmetrical vista opened through the entrance and peristyle towards the main living spaces invite comparison with some of the elite dwellings of first century CE Campania, which used similar architectural devices, and thus raise the possibility that such structures may have played similar roles in both contexts. In some instances visual permeability is matched by physical accessibility. The contrast this represents with earlier Greek structures implies something of a different attitude towards the social norms which seem to have governed interaction between the female members of households and outsiders during the earlier period. If we look more closely at the evidence, however, it becomes clear that the households at Delos did not all follow quite the same social conventions.

A statistical procedure known as cluster analysis can be used to distinguish different groups of houses based on similar values across a range of different characteristics known as variables.[6] Two separate clusters emerge which are defined by the area of ground and number of rooms they include, together with the courtyard form, the amount of decoration and the number of entrances they incorporate (Figure 4.9). While not all of the houses in the sample fall into one of the two, the clusters themselves are coherent and distinctively different from each other, and the differences between the two when other variables are compared suggest further contrasting tendencies. The two clusters can therefore function as guides indicating different trends among separate sets of households. Economic considerations must play some role in separating the two clusters, since ground area, decoration and the presence or absence of a decorative peristyle are three important elements distinguishing them. Availability of resources must

---

[6] For this purpose the file was sorted randomly and the SPSS programme's two-step clustering process was used, which enables both categorical and continuous variables to be analysed. The best solution produced two clusters which described sixty of the houses and were distinguished from each other through a number of different variables. Similar results were achieved with the file sorted in different ways.

Housing and cultural identity

(a) Major Clusters

CLUSTER No.	1 (24 houses)	2 (36 houses)
Ground area (m²) mean/SD[§]	151/57	335/180
Number of entrances: mean/SD	1/0	1.4/0.6
Number of rooms: mean/SD	5.31/1.6	10.13/3.4
Number of decorated rooms: mean/SD	1.5/0.83	3.1/1.75
Frequency of interior painted decoration: figured/plain/none	6/12/6	22/14/0
Frequency of mosaic: patterned/plain/none	0/3/21	12/10/14
Frequency of sculpture: present/absent	4/20	19/17
Courtyard type: single/double	24/0	31/5
Courtyard form: open/anteroom/pastas/peristyle	7/15/2/0	5/7/1/23
Access to upper storey: none or unknown/interior/exterior/both	12/2/9/1	23/5/6/2
Maximum penetration of view from the exterior (mean number of spaces/SD)	1.5/0.83	2/1.12
Depth of decoration from entrance (mean number of spaces/SD)	3/0.88	3.1/1.2

(b) Sub-clusters within Cluster 2

SECONDARY CLUSTER No.	1 (9 houses)	2 (22 houses)
Ground area (m²) mean/SD[§]	407/185	233/95
Number of rooms: mean/SD	10.3/2.8	7.9/3.3
Houses where interior painted decoration visible from street: none/plain/figured	4/2/3	9/12/1
Mosaic emblemata visible from street: no/yes	6/3	21/1
Interior and exterior doorways aligned: no/yes	4/5	20/2
Vista from exterior: none/decorated/symmetrical	4/2/3	15/1/0
Courtyard form: open/anteroom/pastas/peristyle	1/0/0/8	2/5/1/14

[§]SD indicates Standard Deviation, the range of variation around the mean.

Figure 4.9 Tables showing results of the two cluster analyses of the Delos houses: (a) Major clusters; (b) Sub-clusters within Cluster 2

have set parameters, governing the amount of land used and limiting construction materials and decorative features. At the same time the availability of resources must also have influenced the degree to which successive generations of occupants were able to alter or rebuild their houses. But it is still possible to detect other influences which determine how visible decorative features were from the exterior, and which suggest differing conceptions of what a house should be like and the role it should play in the social life of the town.

Of the two clusters, one consists of twenty-four smaller structures ranging between approximately 100 and 200 square metres in ground area and comprising, on average, five interior spaces. These spaces usually included one or two decorated rooms arranged around a single courtyard, which was either open or had a pastas or, more commonly, an enclosed anteroom in front of one or more of the main rooms. Such houses were all accessed from the street via a single entrance. Where a single set of stairs to an upper storey can be traced, these led from the exterior in nine out of eleven cases, suggesting that the upper rooms may often have functioned as separate apartments. While eighteen of the structures in cluster 1 possessed painted plaster walls these were most frequently plain rather than figured, and evidence for patterned mosaics or for sculpture is lacking in most cases. Similarly, as far as we can tell, the façades also seem to have lacked painted decoration. These are not the smallest houses in the town; as noted above, the range of ground areas in the sample as a whole goes as low as 53 square metres, but the smallest houses have few features which can be used effectively to cluster them. Such modestly sized residences probably represent the homes of moderately well-off members of Delian society. What is striking is that in some ways they apparently articulate relatively traditional values: decorative features seem to be for the benefit of residents or visitors entering the houses, but are not aimed at passers-by in the street. At the same time, however, they differ from Greek houses of previous periods in that there is little evidence of a deliberate attempt to screen the entire interior from the street, and in some cases it was possible to see through the entrance into the courtyard and even to look across to sets of rooms beyond. Members of these households therefore seem to have interacted relatively freely with outsiders. A moderate amount of decoration suggests some attention was paid to creating a comfortable living environment and may also indicate that the house played a role as a location for entertaining. Nevertheless, the invisibility of these features from the street suggests that conveying messages about the household's wealth and status to the wider community was not part of their function.

The second cluster represents a strong contrast in several respects: amongst its thirty-six members there is far more variability, both in the scale of the individual structures and in the range of architectural features which they incorporated. The mean area is much larger at 335 square metres, but the standard deviation (the amount of variability around that mean) is also far greater (180 square metres as compared with only 57 square metres in the first cluster). There are a number of other respects in which the houses in this second cluster stand out. The majority have peristyle courtyards, and five include two courtyards within a single house. The entrance arrangements are also sometimes a little different, with all of the houses with multiple street doors falling into this cluster. As with the first cluster, it was often possible to see into these houses from the street outside if the door was left open, but, in contrast with that cluster, here a variety of decorative features were occasionally visible, including the peristyle courts themselves, as well as mosaic emblemata and painted walls. All three of the houses identified above as having symmetrical vistas from the street into the interior fall into this group, and they seem to represent the most extreme examples of a wider trend among the cluster as a whole.

The fact that this second cluster of houses is much more heterogeneous than the first suggests that it encompasses a correspondingly greater variety of ideas about the role a house might play in supporting social life and as a symbol of its inhabitants' outlooks. To explore the nature of those differences further, this second group can be clustered again, highlighting a contrast between nine houses which have a greater mean area but more variation between them and a larger group of nineteen houses which have a lower mean area and lower standard deviation. While the two sub-clusters are similar in many respects, there are significant contrasts in the way in which decorative elements are positioned: among the first sub-cluster mosaic emblemata and painted friezes are frequently visible from the exterior or from the vestibule, and doorways are sometimes aligned, offering a vista through the house. (All three of the houses with axial views, discussed above, fall into this group.) In contrast, in the second sub-cluster, aside from a couple of examples of liturgical paintings on house façades, decorative elements such as painted friezes and mosaic emblemata are visible only very rarely from the exterior or vestibule (one example of each), although all of the houses have wall paintings and five of them also possess mosaic floors. Overall both sub-clusters place emphasis on the use of the domestic environment as a context for display, but the way in which this is done differs: while in a few cases the interior of the house is revealed and placed on view, in the majority the pattern observed amongst the more modestly sized houses applies, with decoration apparently aimed at residents and at visitors actually entering the house, rather than at individuals in the street. The second sub-cluster therefore appears to embody some of the values of the medium-sized houses, but they are applied to larger peristyle structures.

In many modern western towns, housing of different types tends to be zoned according to size and household income, and sometimes also by social and cultural affiliation. This does not seem to have been the case on Delos, where the members of the two major clusters are fairly evenly spread between the different areas represented in the sample. While there is a slight tendency for houses in the Inopos and Skardhana Quarters to be larger and those in the Theatre Quarter to be smaller, this is not sufficiently pronounced to be statistically significant. This is not to say, however, that the houses in the different quarters do not have some distinctive characteristics. The most idiosyncratic area is the Theatre Quarter, where houses tend to be arranged with their rooms leading individually off the courtyard or colonnade, so that the court plays an important role as a circulation space through which it is necessary to pass in order to reach other rooms in the house. The court itself is often left open in this part of town, and there are fewer houses of anteroom or pastas type than one would expect. These characteristics might suggest households living in a relatively traditional manner, following patterns of organisation found in Greece as far back as the Classical period, but other aspects of the houses in this quarter are more innovative: this is one of two areas where houses with two entrances are found, and the houses here also tend to have unusually large numbers of decorated rooms.

Other areas of the town share some characteristics with the Theatre Quarter while contrasting with it in other ways, so that each has a distinctive mix of features. The Inopos Quarter is the only other district which includes some houses with two entrances. At the same time, however, the organisation of space in the houses here tends to be sequential, with suites of rooms entered in series one from another, rather than each opening separately off the court or pastas. The houses of the Skardhana Quarter share this sequential arrangement of rooms and have few open courts. Houses in this area also have more decorated rooms than average. It is this area which is home to both of the triple-entrance houses in the sample. Finally, the area of the House of the Masks is characterised by a prominent role given to the court as a circulation space, which is similar to that in the Theatre Quarter, but the houses here never have more than one entrance.[7]

It is possible that some of these contrasts result from differences in construction date, and while certain features could have been changed (for example a peristyle was sometimes installed within an existing courtyard), others, such as the pattern of circulation, were harder to modify. Although it is impossible to be precise about the construction dates of the houses in all the different areas, the relatively early date of settlement in the Theatre Quarter might explain why this district in particular has patterns of spatial organisation which are characteristically different from those of the other areas. In some cases the presence of multiple entrances and courtyards resulted from combining two, formerly separate, properties, as in the case of Cleopatra and Dioscorides' house. It is interesting, however, that if assessments of the construction sequence are correct, action seems not to have been taken to block duplicate street doors or to reorganise interior space in these houses. As a result there would have been a variety of possible routes into and around the house, making it difficult to supervise the movements of members of the household from a single location. Such a pattern of organisation suggests that, in contrast with the Classical and earlier Hellenistic periods in Greece, control over access to the house and movement around it were not special concerns on Delos at this time. This opening up of the domestic environment is part of a more widespread pattern which is found in other Greek communities by the later second century BCE (Nevett 2002; contra Bonini 2006, who does not quote statistical evidence for his interpretation).

CONCLUSIONS: CULTURAL IDENTITY AND 'IDENTIFICATION'
IN EARLY ROMAN DELOS

These conclusions about the spatial organisation of the houses on Delos suggest the influence of two contrasting sets of expectations about the way in which a house should articulate patterns of intra- and inter-household relationships. In the smaller houses and also in some of the larger ones, the domestic context was conceptualised as essentially a secluded environment in which the character of the interior became evident only to a guest who had come inside. In a second, much smaller, group of large households the interior of the house was deliberately placed on view, demonstrating the

---

[7] Some of these relationships are statistically significant: chi square values for these are as follows: type of courtyard 0.002; number of decorated rooms 0.000; sequential arrangement of rooms 0.000; number of entrances 0.009.

prosperity and perhaps also the status of the occupants through its comfort and refinement, and potentially providing a backdrop against which the householder could appear to the wider community. In crude terms this contrast might be interpreted as evidence for the co-existence of two different cultural groups, since the defining features of each accord well with what we know of some of the main characteristics of Greek and Roman housing traditions. A relatively small number of households occupying some of the large peristyle structures, manipulated the architecture and spatial organisation of their houses in a manner familiar from Italian contexts, most famously from the slightly later houses of Campania, discussed in Chapter 5. While the atrium–peristyle arrangement found so frequently there is not used on Delos, some of the underlying visual language is adopted, with a deliberate symmetry and framing of views from the exterior of the house and between some of the major interior spaces.

At the same time, a larger group of houses seems to express ideals which are more like those of Greek houses from the Classical and earlier Hellenistic periods. This group includes the majority of smaller properties and some larger houses. While it is somewhat simplistic to equate the size of an individual house directly with the economic or social status of its occupants, when the houses are viewed collectively in this way there is likely to be a general relationship between scale and household wealth. Based on this assumption, it seems that the less well-off groups in society were affected somewhat differently by cultural interaction from their elite peers and remained more traditional in their approach to domestic organisation. While such households may have had less access to space and resources, so that adaptating their houses would have been more difficult, an element of choice also seems to have been involved since such households do seem to have emulated styles used by their wealthier peers in installing individual decorative features (Trümper 1998).[8]

Underlying this pattern there is still considerable variation between houses. The clustering procedure isolates different tendencies in the data, but membership of a cluster does not mean that all of the individual houses show every identifying characteristic. What the evidence actually reveals, therefore, is a spectrum of different strategies for using household space, including, in some cases, an ambivalent attitude: the House of Cleopatra and Dioscorides itself is an example of this in that, while the eye is drawn through the street doorway and into the portico of the peristyle, little

---

[8] A comparable argument in support of this kind of emulation has been made for Pompeii during the first century CE: Wallace-Hadrill 1994, 169–174.

of the interior of the house is actually visible. Thus, while the house appears to conform to an idea of transparency and conscious display, in reality it remains relatively enclosed and separated from the outside world. Rather than the creation of a single new 'hybrid' culture, what we seem to see is a mixture of cultural ideals, with individual households actively participating in the process of identification by attempting to strike a balance between contrasting ways of shaping and using domestic space. Analysis of other aspects of the houses suggests that this balance was struck differently in different spheres: for example, preliminary study of domestic ceramic assemblages indicates that households were eager to adopt specifically Italian ways of consuming food and drink (Giros 2000).

Finally, there are also houses which fall outside the range of the two clusters altogether: some of these represent structures which are too small, and therefore have too few characteristic variables, to enable them to be placed reliably in one cluster or another. But there are also some larger houses which do not show the defining characteristics of either of the major clusters. Further study may reveal whether these were influenced more strongly by different sets of cultural ideals, perhaps coming from one or more of the smaller minority groups on the island (for example, traders from the eastern Mediterranean).

CHAPTER 5

Seeking the domus *behind the* dominus *in Roman Pompeii: artefact distributions as evidence for the various social groups*

Bankers and tax collectors should have larger and more beautiful houses, safe from burglars. Public figures and speakers should have elegant and spacious accommodation to receive their visitors. For the true aristocracy who hold office and magistracies, and who must take on state roles, we must build high and stately anterooms, and very spacious atria and peristyles, along with wide groves and walkways completed in a majestic style; in addition we must build libraries, galleries and basilicas fitted out with a magnificence similar to that of public buildings.

Vitruvius, *On Architecture* 6.5.2–3

All members of a society are contributors to the matrix of actions that eventually becomes the archaeological context, and the variety of features is a product of this activity . . . many archaeological features are diffuse, mixed and difficult to interpret. Some, though, are more likely than others to provide information on small group activities; among these are features with rather structured event and/or episode sets, such as houses . . .

Brooks 1982, 68–69

INTRODUCTION

In relative contrast with the houses discussed in the other chapters of this volume, those from the Roman town of Pompeii have been intensively studied for more than 200 years, and it is easy to see why they have attracted so much attention. The Campania region of southern Italy in which they lie was covered in volcanic material by the eruption of Vesuvius in August 79 CE. Today, excavation has revealed about two thirds of the entire town of Pompeii, and it is possible to walk through the streets, wandering in and out of both public buildings and private houses. Walls frequently rise at least one storey and often more, and although the roofs and upper floors have collapsed, the ground floors are frequently relatively complete. The larger houses are adorned with wall paintings, mosaic floors and marble furnishings. Excavators have been able to locate an extensive array of the kinds of everyday items of pottery and metalwork normally present in archaeological contexts, and they have also been able to learn much about some of the fixtures and objects made of organic materials such as wood which are not usually preserved on archaeological sites. The covering of volcanic material at Pompeii is full of voids left behind as those materials rotted away, enabling their original forms to be reconstructed by filling those voids with plaster – a technique which has revealed not only items of furniture such as cupboards and doors, but also the grisly impressions of some of the unluckiest final inhabitants, animal and human, who failed to escape the town's destruction.

The earliest excavations in the houses here and at the neighbouring town of Herculaneum were primarily concerned with recovering mosaics, wall paintings and sculptures, and this, together with the richness of the material itself, encouraged a tendency to study the different architectural elements in isolation. But the Campanian evidence has also been used differently, as a tool for studying social relationships in Roman households, and this is the line of inquiry I want to focus on in this chapter, building on what previous scholars have already achieved. In a landmark paper first published in 1988, Andrew Wallace-Hadrill was one of the first to recognise that ancient houses could be viewed as occupied spaces rather than simply as architectural complexes (Wallace-Hadrill 1988). Since his article was published a generation of scholars have developed and elaborated on many of Wallace-Hadrill's ideas. His discussion builds on the work of earlier researchers who drew a connection between the layout of the larger excavated houses at Pompeii and the kinds of elite residences described by the architect Vitruvius (quoted above), who was writing in Rome during the first century BCE. Among the points Vitruvius makes, two in particular stand out. First, he claims that the type of house a man lived in was expected to be appropriate to his social status. A member of the elite who played a role in public life was expected to receive *clientes* (followers of lower social status, referred to loosely below as 'clients'), business associates and political supporters at his house, and he required a suitable space in which to do this. Second, Vitruvius distinguishes between two different areas of an elite house, one of which was the sole domain of the residents, while the other could be entered by outsiders who had not specifically been invited.

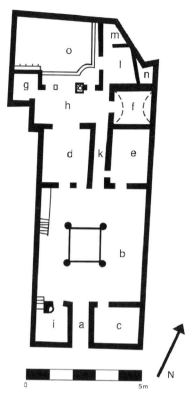

Figure 5.1 Plan of the House of the Ceii (House 1.6.15)

Assisted by additional ancient textual sources, Wallace-Hadrill sketched a detailed model for the way in which Vitruvius' description may have worked at Pompeii, arguing that domestic space can be read as a physical map of social status distinctions. There is much variation in the scale and layout of the individual excavated properties, but the interiors tend to be arranged around two circulation areas, an outer hall and an inner garden (Figures 5.1 to 5.3). Like other scholars before him, Wallace-Hadrill viewed the hall as what Vitruvius called an atrium, but he also looked in detail at how it might have functioned as a space for the formal reception of clients, whose numbers at their patron's house for the morning *salutatio* or greeting were a mark of status and influence. The architecture of the atrium gave it an aura of wealth and power: the ceiling was high, and the decoration and architecture conjured up the impression of a public,

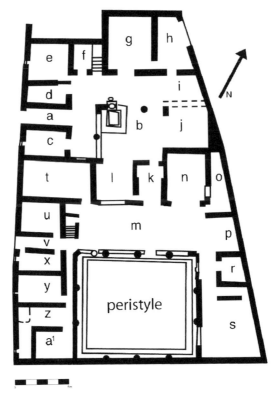

Figure 5.2 Plan of House VI.16.26

rather than a private, building (Plate 5.1). At the rear it gave onto a second room, traditionally referred to by scholars as the tablinum, which had a lower ceiling and sometimes also a raised floor. Here, Wallace-Hadrill suggested, the *dominus* (master of the house) would have been positioned to receive clients in an almost theatrical manner, framed by the architecture. At its rear the tablinum opened into the second circulation space, a garden which often took the form of a colonnaded peristyle. This, Wallace-Hadrill argued (again following Vitruvius), was a more intimate area into which only higher-status associates would have been invited to stroll in the porticoes or dine in decorated triclinia along its sides. He pointed out that service facilities such as storerooms and cooking spaces, which would have been used largely by slaves or servants, were pushed outwards towards the boundaries of the domestic complex and away from this main atrium–peristyle axis, thus marginalising their habitual users.

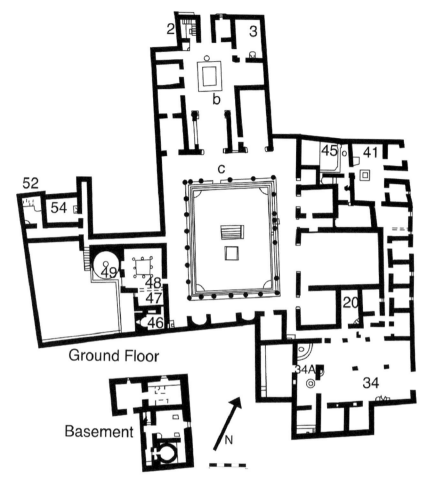

Figure 5.3 Plan of the House of the Menander (House 1.10.4)

This interpretation of the atrium house-form is elegant and has held up well to scrutiny. It is, nevertheless, questionable whether approaching the archaeology through the framework of the texts produces a reliable picture. Several problems with this methodology have been pointed out. One is that, while archaeologists customarily label excavated spaces with Latin names, we cannot be sure that our definitions match those the Roman authors had in mind. This is certainly a difficulty with most room labels, although the identification of atrium and peristyle, on which Wallace-Hadrill's basic argument rests, is fairly secure, thanks to Vitruvius' detailed

Plate 5.1 View into the atrium of the House of the Menander (House 1.10.4), Pompeii

description of these spaces.[1] In addition, the fact that the model maps out a series of conceptual distinctions as well as spatial ones makes the precise identification of functional spaces less crucial to the overall argument. There is, however, a further consequence of using Vitruvius' description as a point of departure in this way that has been less widely acknowledged, but is more troubling, and that is that his particular viewpoint has tended to shape our whole understanding of elite Roman houses. His perspective – that of the *dominus* – is so overwhelming that it is difficult to find evidence anywhere in his text for the roles played by other members of the household,

[1] The dangers of using textual references, from Vitruvius or from any other ancient author, to deduce how rooms may have been used, have been discussed in detail (see Riggsby 1997; Allison 2004, 161–177). See Chapter 1 for further discussion of the potential problems in trying to use ancient texts to understand the use of household space.

including its women (compare Milnor 2005, 107). Of course, this bias is part of a wider cultural and social universe in which elite male discourse predominated. One strength of taking a material cultural approach to the social dynamics of Pompeian houses should be that we can look beyond that dominant discourse to explore alternative viewpoints and other social roles. The few attempts that have been made to investigate the activities of particular social groups such as women and slaves in these households have had mixed success. Viewing the household through the lens of Vitruvius, and hence from the perspective of the *dominus*, has led to the conclusion that the influence of these groups was relatively unimportant since they had little effect on the physical organisation of the central axis of the house (for example Wallace-Hadrill 1996; George 1997). From this perspective other members of the household are detectable only in the interstices of the *dominus'* world. But do we get a different view if we try to approach the archaeological evidence directly?

A major study by Penelope Allison was aimed at clarifying the way in which individual spaces in Pompeian houses were used (Allison 2004). A particular strength of Allison's work is that, as well as looking at the architecture and decoration of the houses, she also explored in detail the types and distribution of the many objects found in different rooms. Where sufficient information was available, she recorded where in the room each item was located and how deeply it was buried, important details which can reveal that objects may have been used or stored together, or whether they may have fallen from an upstairs room as the upper storeys of houses collapsed under the weight of accumulating volcanic material. Excavators must have missed some items and been selective about what they recorded, so that this kind of database can offer only a partial picture of what the houses originally contained. Even so, putting together a comprehensive list is a daunting task: in Allison's sample of thirty houses there were 865 rooms which together contained over 16,000 artefacts. Many problems and inconsistencies in the material emerged which are routinely overlooked: some houses showed evidence that redecoration or construction work was under way, hindering any attempt to understand how those properties functioned as living spaces; elsewhere, rooms with elaborate wall decoration contained mundane domestic artefacts, or no artefacts at all; and many spaces contained motley assortments of items with a wide range of different uses. For those accustomed to Wallace-Hadrill's *dominus*-centred model, Allison's study revealed some interesting results: for example, the atrium was shown to be not only a monumental reception space for the use of the *dominus* and his visitors, but also a location where a variety of domestic items such as loom weights and table vessels were kept, revealing the presence of other members of the household here as well. Ultimately, however, the volume and diversity of information resulting from this study are difficult to digest, and Allison's complete renunciation of textual evidence made questions about patterns of social behaviour impossible for her to address (Allison 2004, 154–158).

A question that remains, then, is whether it is possible to use the material from Pompeii to build a model of domestic organisation which gives more weight to the other members of the household besides the *dominus*, and which combines the evidence of texts and archaeology in a more balanced manner. Recent studies in the archaeology of other periods and regions have pointed out that the best place to search for the influence of less empowered groups like women, servants and children is in the kind of artefactual material Allison has brought together, since this is evidence for the kinds of small-scale, short-term activities over which such individuals are likely to have had most control (Gilchrist 2000, 325–326). In both Greek and Roman contexts the focus of most artefact analysis has been on isolating the functions of different rooms, but to date studies of artefact distributions have often been seen as frustratingly inconclusive (for example Foxhall 2000; Cahill 2002, 70–72). Even where both architecture and finds have been well preserved and relatively well documented, as at Pompeii, the task of pinpointing a single dominant activity in a specific architectural space has proved difficult, and this has led some scholars to suggest that the individual room is too small as a unit of analysis (Berry 1997, 194), while others have questioned whether much at all can be learned about Roman society from studying artefact distributions (see for example the contributions in Vanhaverbeke *et al.* 2008).

One response to this problem has been a more critical approach to the natural and human processes which have shaped the archaeological site since the houses were left by their occupants (known as site formation processes). Even at a site such as Pompeii, which was rapidly abandoned, we cannot expect the distribution of artefacts to be unaffected by the circumstances surrounding the site's destruction. In fact detailed study of the architecture has revealed extensive evidence for re-entry to buildings during or after the eruption. Holes in many walls reveal escape routes or the passage of intruders, and messages scrawled on house exteriors indicate the activities of rescue parties or looters.[2] In addition, for some years before the final eruption in 79 CE there were earthquakes, including a

---

[2] For example CIL IV 2311, on the exterior of house VII.2.20, which reads 'House tunnelled through': Cooley and Cooley 2004, 40.

serious one in 62 CE which is known from preserved textual sources to have caused severe damage to public buildings and presumably damaged private houses as well. It has often been argued that earthquakes led to the repair, modification and even the abandonment of some houses prior to the final eruption, although Allison's analysis suggested that at least some of the properties in her sample were still inhabited at the time of the destruction (Allison 2004, 192–196). Whenever the houses were abandoned, it is likely that their inhabitants would have had an opportunity to store or to carry away some prized possessions, and we should not discount the potentially disruptive influence of these kinds of activities. The effect of the eruption in distorting (rather than reducing) the artefact assemblages should therefore not be underestimated, and study of a variety of houses at other ancient sites has found similar levels of apparent disorganisation, even though the circumstances of their abandonment were different. As with domestic structures whose occupants may have departed for other reasons and sometimes less hastily, some possessions may have been carried away from Pompeii by its fleeing population while others may have been gathered together or hoarded in the hope of an eventual return. Before using artefact distributions as evidence for patterns of activity, it is therefore important to ask whether we can make more sense of the objects that were found and recorded by thinking systematically and in detail about these and some of the other processes which may have structured their deposition.

FLEXIBILITY AND MULTIFUNCTIONALITY IN THE USE OF DOMESTIC SPACE AT POMPEII

The common focus on the role of the *dominus* in shaping the domestic environment at Pompeii has tended to emphasise a number of aspects of elite domestic culture which appear to be uniquely 'Roman'. Indeed it has been explicitly argued that the architecture of Pompeian houses, and others outside Italy in a number of the provinces, deliberately projected an image of the 'Romanitas' or 'Roman-ness' of their owners (Hales 2003, *passim*). In a variety of practical ways, however, Roman housing from Pompeii and elsewhere has much in common not only with that of Classical Greece but also with dwellings from a range of pre-modern and non-western societies which have been studied through archaeological, historical and ethnographic work. Such studies suggest that the present-day western concern for providing specialised rooms for particular activities and for allocating separate spaces to different members of the household is a relatively recent phenomenon which has developed as a consequence of the rise of 'individualism' in western thought. In most societies, at most times, a single space has tended to be multifunctional and to be used by a number of different household members. At the same time, analysis of significant numbers of Latin, and also Greek, texts making reference to domestic activities suggests that in both Greek and Roman societies space was perceived as potentially flexible, its use changing dependent on a variety of factors. Among these seasonality was particularly significant since changes in sunlight and temperature had implications for how warm or cool rooms facing in different directions could be (Nevett 1997, Nevett 1999, 36). These characteristics of ancient domestic behaviour have been acknowledged by classical archaeologists looking at artefact distributions in both Greek and Roman contexts (for example Berry 1997; Foxhall 2000). Nevertheless, the extent, nature and implications of flexibility in spatial use in ancient houses have remained largely unexplored.

Here, then, my goal is to investigate evidence for flexibility in the use of space at Pompeii by identifying systematic patterns of variation which may underlie artefact distributions. These are used as a basis for detecting some of the relatively small-scale, short-term patterns of domestic activity which should tell us most about the less privileged members of these households. In the process I highlight some of the assumptions that need to be made about how artefact distributions are likely to relate to patterns of behaviour, and I make explicit use of some of the models for interpreting these relationships outlined by the anthropologist Michael Schiffer based on ethnographic studies (Schiffer 1996). Although the artefacts are the main focus, they are viewed as part of a wider complex of information which also includes the provenience (the location in which they were found) together with any architectural and decorative features which help to provide a context.

Three different aspects of the evidence potentially show multifunctional or flexible use of space: the first, and most commonly observed phenomenon in both Roman and Greek contexts, is the occurrence of artefacts and/or architectural features used for two or more different activities in the same physical area; this is balanced by a second, closely linked, phenomenon, more rarely discussed, which is that evidence for the same activity is sometimes found in two or more different areas and may indicate flexibility in spatial usage; a third and final pattern merits separate consideration, and that is an apparent incompatibility in the activities suggested by the architecture and decoration of a space, and the objects found there. These configurations result from the kinds of small-scale activities carried out by individuals or small groups over a short period of time (Brooks 1982, 68). As examples through which to explore these indicators of the flexible use of space, I discuss in detail three specific atrium-type houses, the House of the Ceii (1.6.15), House VI.16.26 and the House of the Menander (1.10.4). In all three cases the excavators not only recorded many of the finds but also attempted to distinguish items that were in storage from those that may have been in use at the time of the destruction.[3] Although they are all atrium-type buildings they represent a range of different sizes, with ground areas of roughly 300, 600 and 1,800 square metres respectively. While these houses obviously do not constitute a statistically significant sample for generalising about the use of domestic space across the town of Pompeii as a whole, they do provide insights into multifunctionality and flexibility of spatial use, and there are some similarities between them which may be indicative of broader patterns.

In the House of the Ceii (named by modern scholars after two brothers whom they thought once occupied it) the major phase of construction is dated to the second half of the second century BCE, although the house incorporates earlier walls and also shows signs of some later modification (Figure 5.1). Eleven rooms are arranged around an atrium (b) at the front and a small garden at the rear (o) (Figure 5.1). Holes dug through the walls in several places seem to indicate the movements of escapees or looters at the time of the eruption. Allison comments that the assemblage is very mixed, containing relatively few movable finds and much evidence of empty storage cupboards, all of which she suggests are the result of events during the abandonment of the town, when items were carried away or salvaged (Allison, date unknown).

House VI.16.26 consists of twenty-two rooms organised around an atrium (b) and a compact peristyle (Figure 5.2). The atrium appears to have had an unusual design, with a large open area to the south-east, and porticoes to north and west. The peristyle has a deep ambulatory to its north side and shallower ones to its east and west, of which the western one was walled in to create a corridor. On the fourth, southern, side the central garden space is delimited by a wall, but engaged columns create the visual

---

[3] I build directly here on the information gathered and summarised by Allison, whose work provides the best picture we have of the artefactual contents of Pompeian houses and their spatial distribution. However, I do occasionally differ from her in interpreting the use to which an object may have been put (for example, I take small glass bottles/flasks to be toilet or table items, rather than transport vessels). Assigning functions to specific objects is not a scientific process since they may not always have been used for the purpose for which they were made, or indeed may have been made to cater to a variety of uses. Assessments of whether an item was being used, stored or discarded are also subjective, depending on interpretation of contextual information.

effect of a full peristyle. Contrary to the stereotypical view, in this house the atrium and peristyle lie side-by-side rather than one behind the other. Also, somewhat atypically, there is no evidence for elaborate wall painting. Allison suggests that the area around the peristyle may have been abandoned since it appears to have yielded few finds. A pile of roofing tiles in the atrium suggests that renovation work may have been planned or under way here at the time of the eruption. Moving between these two areas would have necessitated passing through one of the rooms facing onto the peristyle, since the large room l, which is reminiscent of a transitional tablinum space, seems to have been walled in at the back with only a window looking out towards the peristyle. Both northern and southern areas of the building had their own street entrances, and it is therefore a possibility that the two were occupied separately, at least for part of the life of the house.

The well-known House of the Menander (named by modern scholars after a painting of the famous fourth-century Greek comic playwright on the wall of one of its rooms) is unusually complex in its pattern of organisation (Figure 5.3), owing to its large size, but its relatively recent excavation means that it provides particularly detailed information about movable finds. Like the House of the Ceii, in-depth study of the architecture suggests that this house developed into its present form over a period of several centuries. It also grew considerably, incorporating parts of neighbouring properties (Ling 1997, 52–59, 223–237). The original nucleus of the house, the atrium (b) and surrounding rooms, perhaps with a garden behind, has been dated to the late third to mid second century BCE. By the time of the destruction the property comprised some fifty different rooms, including additional courtyard and garden spaces to east, south-east and west of the main atrium–peristyle axis (b–c), a second atrium to the east of the peristyle (41), and a bath suite along with four basement rooms on the west side (46–49). In his published summary of the architecture and history of the insula Ling commented that there was extensive evidence of earthquake damage (Ling 1997, 234–237). Redecoration was evidently taking place in several rooms, and work seems to have been under way to modernise the furnace in the bath suite (Ling 1997, 135). There were, nonetheless, large numbers of artefacts in the house at the time of the destruction, suggesting that any interruption in occupation was not anticipated to be lengthy. In fact during excavation of the corridor south-east of the peristyle, skeletal remains were recovered from a group of at least nine individuals who included three children under five (Lazer 1997). It is unclear whether the owner of the house and his family were in residence at the time of the eruption, whether these were slaves or servants taking care of the property while it was renovated or whether they were outsiders seeking refuge.

Evidence for two or more activities taking place in a single space, and for the use of several different spaces for the same activity

The characteristic mixing of material associated with a variety of activities taking place within a single architectural space is widespread in all three houses. As the work of Michael Schiffer suggests (Schiffer 1996), a first step in interpreting the artefactual evidence is to try to establish, as far as possible, whether individual items were left behind where they were actually used, or whether they were in storage or had been set aside for discard or recycling.

Refuse is the category of evidence most difficult to identify for a variety of reasons, not least because definitions of rubbish are subjective. Today an item of rubbish could be seen as something no longer needed or wanted by its owner. In pre-modern societies, though, rates of discard were much lower. This is partly because in such societies people had fewer possessions – particularly disposable ones (Deetz 1977, 59). But it is also because a scarcity of resources meant that items tended to be repaired, reused for other purposes or recycled to make new objects. Evidence of this in Greek and Roman contexts can be seen in the number of excavated ceramic vessels which have been mended in Antiquity. A couple of criteria can be used to define refuse: first, its context, which may suggest that objects had been gathered together to be discarded or that they had already entered a rubbish deposit; and second, its condition, which may have been damaged or fragmentary at the time it was deposited (although it should be borne in mind that ethnographic work has shown that broken items are sometimes reused for a different purpose: Schiffer 1996, 30–32).

At sites such as Pompeii, where many structures were excavated a long time ago and there was a wealth of architectural and other information to be recorded, fragmentary items and rubbish deposits have often tended to be overlooked or given low priority. Nevertheless, given the likelihood of the preferential recording of valuable items, one practice to look for is the hoarding of discarded items, which in societies where resources are scarce are often kept as potential raw materials for future reuse – a phenomenon that Schiffer refers to as 'clutter refuse' (Schiffer 1996, 66). The fact that such pieces should be categorised as discarded, rather than in use, is not necessarily always obvious because identification relies on precise and accurate information about their context and on a judgement about whether or not any breakages occurred before the eruption. Nevertheless, there are a few instances in which the inventories of our example houses seem to include examples of this kind of clutter refuse.

In various locations in the House of the Menander and the House of the Ceii fragments of marble sculpture were found, apparently already broken before the eruption. Allison suggests that 'unless their provenances were the result of post-eruption disturbance, they are . . . evidence of pre-eruption dislocation and disturbance' (Allison 2004, 39). But this is not always borne out by their contexts. For example, in the secondary atrium of the House of the Menander (room 41) a marble arm seems to have been stored on a shelf along with a variety of other objects. This location, together with the fact that the room seems to have been a service area (see below), implies that the arm had perhaps been here for a while, possibly salvaged at some point by the users of this area for reuse or sale. A similar case in the House of the Ceii involves two broken pieces of marble sculpture found in room i, which seems to have been temporarily disused at the time of the eruption and might therefore have been particularly suitable for keeping such clutter refuse. A complete Egyptian-style marble figurine found in the fill of room z of House VI.16.26 may also fall into this category. The association between marble objects, often in fragmentary state, and cooking areas is in fact more widespread in Allison's sample. For example, the House of the Vettii, another large, well-decorated house, also contained fragmentary sculpture in hearth room w. The presence of such objects in these rooms reinforces the suggestion that they were being hoarded as a potentially valuable resource, perhaps having been scavenged by lower-status individuals working here.

A different form of recycling can be documented in relation to some of the large amphorae which were used to transport and store foodstuffs. Considerable numbers of these vessels were found in the House of the Menander, some bearing dipinti (painted lettering) which noted their contents. In one case a vessel whose original label stated that it contained local wine had been relabelled indicating that it had been refilled with vinegar. Another group of wine amphorae found in the secondary atrium on the east side of the house contained stucco, lime used for plastering, and signinum powder used for making floors (Stefani 2003b, 210–211). Even broken amphorae could be useful: Allison suggests that amphora toes were used to support round-bottomed cooking pots (Allison 2004, 101).

In addition to clutter refuse and recycling, there are also a couple of instances where excavators do seem to have been dealing with, and to have recorded, deposits of discarded refuse. These are a cistern beneath the floor in the House of the Menander corridor l, and a walled-up ground floor space in the House of the Ceii (n). These structures contained a number of fragments of fine terra sigillata pottery and other ceramic vessels, as well as sherds from lamps and glassware, all of which had presumably been broken in use, cleared up, and discarded here. In the House of the Menander these were combined with plant matter, and even a coin and four finger rings.[4]

By contrast with the recycling and disposal of rubbish, which we can only glimpse occasionally in the recorded evidence, storage is the most widely represented activity: in the House of the Ceii, for example, evidence for storage of one sort or another was noted in six of the thirteen spaces. The atrium alone housed at least three separate storage structures: a set of shelves under the stairs contained a mixed assemblage including tableware and lamps; a cupboard in the south-east corner, preserved as a plaster cast, held toilet articles, while a chest in the north-east corner contained a single cup. A further concentration of stored items was located in room g, which was lined with shelves and cupboards or chests. Table vessels were found in this area, too, alongside iron tools and a casket for valuables. The varied collection of items in this room is in keeping with Schiffer's cross-cultural observation that storage areas tend to be cleared out relatively rarely, and that they therefore accumulate mixed assortments of possessions (Schiffer 1996, 68–69). In cases like the atrium of the House of the Ceii, such stored assemblages can account for a particularly wide range of objects with different uses occurring together in a single room. Storage patterns are not completely random, however: within the atrium a distinction seems to have been made between tableware and toilet items, and across the house as a whole there is some degree of specialisation in terms of what is kept where: tools are stored only in room g and toilet items only in the atrium, while tableware is kept in the atrium and room g. A similar pattern occurs in House VI.16.26, where evidence for food storage is found only in the atrium and peristyle, storage of personal items is located only in rooms e and k, and evidence for storage of table-ware is limited to rooms l and f.

---

[4] Room n in the House of the Ceii may have been linked with a toilet in an upper storey and was excavated in 1983 connection with the publication of the house (Michel 1990, 63). House of the Menander corridor l is referred to by Ling as room P: Ling and Clarke 1997, 274. The presence here of whole vessels as well as fragments led Allison to suggest that it was not a rubbish deposit (Allison, date unknown). Whole vessels are sometimes found in wells and cisterns where they have been lost in the process of drawing water. The inclusion of a bowl full of hazelnuts is admittedly curious, but the amount of fragmentary material suggests that some of this deposit, at least, does constitute refuse. It is perhaps possible that some of the other items were left behind during the construction of the cistern or, as Allison suggests elsewhere, that it was some sort of foundation deposit (Allison 2004, 130).

The House of the Menander echoes these distinctions on a larger scale, although tableware and personal items are recorded only as being stored in a small number of rooms. An exceptional find came from the basement area on the west side of the house, where the remains of a wooden chest were found to contain 118 pieces of silver tableware which had been carefully wrapped for storage in heavy cloth and were hence very well preserved. In the chest with them was found a smaller wooden box containing some gold jewellery and gold and silver coins, suggesting that this was a hoard that had been hidden away with the hope of recovering it at a later date.[5] A group of bronze table vessels were found in a second chest on the other side of the room and additional bronze vessels seem to have been placed directly on the floor of the room.

There are a number of locations in each house in which evidence was recorded of storage structures but where only a few items are noted as having been stored, and sometimes there is no note of any stored item being recovered at all (for example, in rooms e and l in the House of the Ceii).[6] If we could safely assume that everything once kept in these houses is likely to have been preserved, excavated and recorded, then the amount of unused capacity would suggest that the occupants took away many of their possessions. But such an assumption is unwarranted: the relatively small assemblages of ceramic food preparation-, table- and cooking-wares recovered from all three properties suggest the possibility that some of the more mundane finds in these categories may not have been noted by the excavators if they were in fragmentary condition. (In the House of the Ceii, for instance, fewer than ten small, open vessels which could have been used for drinking are recorded from the entire ground floor of the house.) Finds of a limited number of complete vessels, together with the contents of the refuse deposits in the House of the Menander and the House of the Ceii mentioned above, reinforce the evidence for the use of fine terra sigillata pottery and other ceramic vessels in the two houses, and the sherds of such vessels, broken as the city was destroyed, may often have been disregarded by the excavators. It is also relevant to think about what kinds of organic materials are likely to have been in use in the house but will not have survived at all, since these may account for at least some of this empty

---

[5] The latest coins date to 78 or 79 CE suggesting that they were placed here at the time of the eruption or shortly beforehand, although this does not necessarily mean that the silver, which was on the bottom of the chest, had not been there for longer (Painter 2001, 12).

[6] These are identifiable as niches, remnants of fitments and fittings, or as casts, although items recorded as door fittings are excluded from my consideration on the basis that they could indicate room doors rather than pieces of furniture. My selection therefore represents a minimum number.

space. A major category of bulky item rarely recovered at Pompeii is cloth: woollen blankets would have been required for night-time use in winter, and these are likely to have been stored away at the time of the eruption in August, perhaps along with extra layers of warm clothing also for winter use.

A second type of organic material which may be under-represented in some of the houses is basic foodstuffs, both liquid, such as wine and olive oil, and solid, such as flour. There is evidence for large amounts of storage and/or consumption of liquids in the House of the Menander, where numerous amphorae were found in a variety of different areas including the stable-courtyard (34), rooms off the peristyle and the basement under the bath suite. Many of the shapes are those of wine amphorae and they show that the vessels had once contained both local wines and also imports from Crete and Rhodes. The dipinti carried by some of them specified that they also held other products including olive oil, honey and Spanish *liquamen* (a form of *garum* or fish sauce) (Stefani 2003b, 210–211). Liquids could also have been kept in smaller vessels, like the coarse ware jug, 25 cm tall, found in the secondary atrium and labelled with a dipinto giving its contents as vinegar (Fergola 2003, 165–166). These containers offer some indication of the variety of foodstuffs which might have been consumed in a household such as this, although the evidence for recycling, noted above, makes it unclear how many full ones would have been kept on hand at any one time. It is possible that at the time of the destruction some of them were clutter refuse. A likely example is a group of forty-three amphorae which were stacked together against the wall in a corner of the stable-courtyard in such a way that most would have been inaccessible had anyone wanted to get at their contents.

The household must have prepared and consumed staples such as grain, since several hand querns for processing it were found in the house. But this is likely to have been supplemented by pre-prepared foods, such as bread from local bakeries which were equipped for large-scale production. We currently know little about general consumption patterns and the balance between home-produced and bought-in products is likely to have varied between households. Direct evidence for storage of dry goods in the house is lacking, and these were perhaps kept in sacks or cloth bags which were not preserved. Comparable evidence for storage of foodstuffs is also present in House vi.16.26 in the form of amphorae and large dolia or storage jars, which were kept in the peristyle. In the House of the Ceii three amphorae were found in room i, and smaller vessels and/or dry foods in sacks or bags could have occupied some of the empty cupboard space in this room.

The smaller size of this house is likely to have meant that there were fewer people here to feed, and more limited space to accumulate clutter refuse such as empty amphorae, although more amphorae were present amongst material found above floor level in room d, which may have fallen from upper-storey rooms.

To some extent, then, recycling and storage patterns help to explain some of the mixture of activities apparently attested in many rooms. But this raises a further question: where were these stored items used? Of course, we cannot answer this for sure, but it is possible to make some suggestions based on the proximity to each other of items used for associated tasks and on the distribution of items which seem to have been left out in rooms, rather than stored away.[7] An example are the related groups of objects associated with storing, preparing, cooking and consuming food and drink already mentioned, which are relatively straightforward to identify even if it is not always possible to be precise about the stage (or stages) they facilitated in the journey of food and drink from store to table. Room i in the House of the Ceii, where the three amphorae were found, was also furnished with a fixed hearth which was probably used for cooking. In the House of the Menander a room in a similar location and with a similar structure (room 3) may also have been used this way. It is easy to see that, given the size and location of these rooms, the atrium was the convenient place to store bulk foods that could not be accommodated in the hearth room itself. A similar arrangement seems to have prevailed in House VI.16.26, where a hearth room (z) was located at the rear, opening onto the peristyle. An additional hearth which may also have been used for cooking was found in nearby room t.

A mystery is the lack of cooking pottery in or close to any of these hearth rooms: this could reflect selectivity on the part of the excavators, but, as Allison suggests, it could also indicate that none was actually being used for cooking immediately prior to the eruption. If any of the three houses was still occupied at that time, then cooking may have taken place elsewhere in the building. The House of the Ceii was equipped with a bronze brazier found in room l (off the garden) which could have been used for this purpose. Seasonal variation in day-length and temperature

---

[7] It is important to remember that the assemblages noted in the excavation reports as being in storage are likely to represent a minimum: at least some of the objects whose contexts are not noted or which were thought to have come from the floor may actually have been in or on pieces of furniture, the presence of which was not detected or noted. I am excluding from consideration objects noted by Allison as likely to have come from upper storeys: while these are important evidence of the kinds of activities which may have been carried out in upstairs rooms, their lack of context makes them more difficult to use for the questions I am trying to address here.

must have been a major influence on patterns of activity, even in the largest, wealthiest houses. In recent years mean temperatures in Campania have varied between a minimum of close to 0° C in January and a high of almost 30° C in July and August, and individual days can be somewhat hotter (or colder). The range in Antiquity is likely to have been similar. In the absence of effective artificial heating and lighting, the most efficient strategy for coping with this kind of variation would have been to use different rooms at different times of day and during different seasons. This would have enabled the occupants of the house to take advantage of the warmth and light provided by a low sun in winter, or exclude the hot sunlight and capture breezes in summer.

The importance of this kind of seasonality in both Greek and Roman Antiquity is supported by a variety of references made in the ancient sources to the need for adapting architectural design to take sunlight into account at different times of year (for example, Varro, *On the Latin Language* 8.29.4 and Cicero, *Letters to his Brother Quintus* 3.1.2). Since Pompeii was destroyed in August, it seems possible that hearth rooms were used more in winter months, when the heat would have been an asset, whereas during the summer food was cooked on braziers which could be carried to the best-ventilated locations and would not have overheated the interior. In the summer months, then, light cooking which did not require lighting a whole oven may have been the norm. Such meals could have been supplemented by baked goods bought from one of the many commercial bakeries in the town. The evidence from the House of the Menander suggests that this pattern may have been followed even in large houses where slaves may have been able to prepare food well away from the apartments occupied by the householder.

In the House of the Menander a decorative bronze brazier with lion feet and lion head fittings was found in the peristyle itself, and a plainer iron one in an alcove on its south wall. But the situation here was more complicated. As well as the front hearth room (3), several other spaces in the house were furnished with similar built-in hearth features (including rooms 20, 34A, 41, 45, 52 and 54). There has been some debate about how many were used for cooking and whether others may have had heating or craft purposes, but it may not make sense to try to separate these different uses too rigidly: a single hearth could potentially have been used in different ways. In most cases there was little trace of any cooking or food-preparation equipment associated with these structures, suggesting that they, also, may not have been in use in August 79 CE. Again, it is possible that during the colder winter months several of the ovens/furnaces operated at once to warm different parts of the structure, and perhaps to cook food for different groups of occupants. Allison raises the possibility that the side atrium (41) and surrounding rooms may have been occupied by a household separate from the one living in main part of the house, although the overall pattern of organisation suggests that at one time, at least, the whole house did function as a single residential unit (Ling 1997, 105–118). Alongside the core atrium–peristyle axis was the bath area to the west, together with a hearth room which, during the winter months, may have served those who worked here. To the east, further rooms are arranged around the secondary atrium (41), the stable-courtyard (34), and the corridor which connects the two (l). These make sense as service quarters: the secondary atrium and surrounding rooms contained a variety of different artefacts, some, such as a decorated couch, seemingly quite expensive. But these were combined with utilitarian household items, suggesting that a few choice pieces may have been scrounged from the main part of the house when no longer required and hoarded by those whose lives were centred in these rooms. The stable-courtyard in this area, with its cart, was perhaps used for provisioning a large household, although Allison suggests that it may have fallen into disuse prior to the eruption.

How do patterns of consumption relate to this picture of food preparation? Vessels will be found where they were used, giving an indication of dining areas, only if the dishes from the last meal taken in a space were left behind and not cleared away. This means that in order to get a fuller picture it is helpful to look at how the distribution of any serving vessels from the house floors may relate to those in storage. In the House of the Ceii tableware stored both at the front of the house in the atrium and at the rear, in room g, is likely to indicate patterns of dining rather than food preparation: the shapes of the majority of vessels suggest they were used for drinking, and they are therefore likely to have been filled where dining was taking place. The binary pattern of storage suggests that, in common with cooking, dining may also have moved seasonally, or even at different times of the day, between the front part of the house and the rear.

In large houses like the House of the Menander, rooms with comparable dimensions which could have been used for dining are duplicated, with examples leading off both atrium and peristyle, facing in different directions, and varying in the extent to which they are open to the outside. In winter, those facing south across an open peristyle would have been lighted and warmed by the rays of the low sun for much of the day, while others on the north side would have avoided the sun and remained cooler for summer use. Similarly, at midday during the summer the atrium may have acted as a reservoir for cool air, shaded and with the double height ceiling allowing hot air to rise. Rooms leading off here may have been cooler at this time of day than those giving directly onto the peristyle. Vitruvius specifically recommended using different rooms for dining at different times of the year.[8] A similar consideration probably also lies behind some of the more uncommon names applied to domestic spaces mentioned in the texts: for example, *hibernacula* (literally, little winter places), perhaps easier to heat than larger ones which may have been used in summer. Such a wide range of alternative venues would not have been available in smaller houses like the House of the Ceii; nevertheless, even the occupants of this house may still have had some choice of locations with different thermal properties which they could have used for dining and other activities. Decorated rooms (c) and (e), which opened off the atrium, perhaps provided warm, sheltered spaces in winter; a further, smaller, decorated room (f) faced west onto the ambulatory and may have received more ventilation from the garden; a larger, undecorated, room (d) faced north onto the ambulatory and looked out over the garden beyond (o) through a wide opening.

In the House of the Menander evidence for consumption in the form of serving vessels is widespread. Only in two rooms are caches of such items noted specifically as being in storage, as opposed to in usage contexts. One of these is the set of silverware and the bronze vessels from the basement mentioned earlier. The other consists of two groups of serving vessels of various types in glass, ceramic and bronze, which were stored on a shelf and inside a chest in the secondary atrium (41), along with various other kinds of objects such as toilet articles. A mixture of cooking pots and further serving vessels was recovered from the floor of the same room and may indicate the use of such vessels there. Serving vessels which appear to have been found where they were used are also noted from a number of other locations in the house. Of the rooms in the atrium complex facing either inwards into the atrium itself, or south into the peristyle, half had at least one such vessel: mostly these were small, isolated ceramic cups, plates or lids, although room 2 held a cache of sixteen ceramic dishes. A couple of bronze vessels also came from this area, but the amount of pottery is striking in comparison with what is recorded from the other two houses. Rather than representing a real difference, this may simply

---

[8] Vitruvius, *On Architecture* 6.4.1–2.

suggest that greater attention was paid to recording such items on the part of the excavators of this house. It also seems surprising in the light of the concentration of bronze vessels which, although they might be assumed to be more valuable, were found in the secondary atrium (41), an area which may have been associated with food preparation by slaves and servants. One potential explanation for this apparent anomaly is that the cache of silver and bronze in the basement represents a collection of more valuable table items gathered up from the rooms around the atrium and peristyle, where they may have been used instead of, or alongside, pottery. In his publication of the silver plate, Kenneth Painter argues that the collection represented eight place settings, and points out that this number is suited to formal dining outdoors, rather than to indoor banquets, where couches were normally set up to hold groups of six or nine diners. Nevertheless, he also raises the possibility that there was a special dining set for the *dominus* himself, which may have included vessels of gold and/or precious stones, and which was not stored along with the silver (Painter 2001, 40–41). If this were the case, then a set of eight place settings to complement it would make perfect sense for dining indoors.

The small numbers and wide distribution of the ceramic items suggest the possibility that some may have been the residue of food and drink taken in different rooms and not cleared away before the abandonment of the house. (Comparable untidiness before the abandonment of a house has been observed in other cultural contexts: Schiffer 1996, 97–98.) Their widespread occurrence raises a question about modes of consumption in such large, wealthy households outside the formal banquet or *cena*. If they were resident at the time of the eruption, is it possible that the owner and his family may have eaten separately or in small groups, rather than together? Or were the dishes left here by caretakers or workmen taking refreshments as they redecorated or cleaned the rooms in which they were found? Again, our knowledge of the context and condition of these items, and of what may originally have lain alongside them, is not sufficient to justify a conclusion, but this is a question that might be addressed through future research into more informal patterns of consumption.

Cases where the evidence appears to indicate incompatible activities
taking place in a single space

Another phenomenon which creates an appearance of disorder is the apparent incompatibility between different elements of the architecture of a space and/or the objects found in it. This can take different forms, and there are therefore a number of potential explanations. In general terms, discussion of this phenomenon has often been focused on the effects of the eruption and preceding seismic activity, associating these events with structural damage and with consequent changes in patterns of use. While the consequences of such events must, of course, be considered, there are also other reasons why we might perceive the evidence as contradictory, some of which result from our own cultural expectations about what activities may share a single space, while others are linked to the way in which both the houses themselves, and the composition of the households occupying them, changed through time.

Perhaps the most commonly cited instance of this kind of contradictory evidence is where rooms whose décor suggests that they may have been intended as reception or living rooms contain items which are more mundane and functional. A striking example is the atrium. Superficially, if these spaces are viewed from the Vitruvian perspective as reception areas designed to fit the needs of the *dominus,* then the discovery of a piece of storage furniture together with an amphora in the atrium of the House of the Menander, alongside its carefully executed wall paintings, seems anomalous. Similarly anomalous are the three different storage features in the painted atrium of the House of the Ceii. As argued earlier in this chapter, however, storage was a major feature of these houses, and the presence of this and other forms of domestic activity pervades the atrium–peristyle axis just as much as the outer or rear 'service' areas. There must have been a practical advantage, in that the wide space of the atrium was suitable for accommodating large pieces of furniture and storage vessels. This must have been even truer of the peristyle and garden spaces, which were the only possible locations for keeping even larger storage vessels like the dolia in the peristyle of House VI.16.26. Storage in such visible locations might have been a deterrent against pilfering of food. The atrium was used for storage even in the House of the Menander, where the numerous rooms and variety of courtyards provided alternative space for such items.

It therefore seems that, contrary to what we might assume, amphorae, chests and other storage equipment were not something to hide away so as not to spoil the gracious effect of architecture and wall paintings. Instead it is likely that they were considered not to detract from the overall effect and possibly even to contribute positively to it in some way, perhaps as evidence to visitors that the house was well supplied and organised in an orderly fashion. Such an interpretation would be consistent with some of the symbolism attached to the atrium in various textual sources, where it is seen as the traditional core of the house, the main living space, whose features accommodated some of the most important aspects of domestic activity. This, the writers claim, was the original location of the main domestic hearth and the room where the marriage bed of the *dominus* was placed. In addition it was a centre for domestic worship at the household altar, and the location in which a variety of events such as religious festivals, births, marriages and deaths would all have been celebrated or commemorated (Flower 1995, 194–203; Nevett 1997, 290). These sources may not necessarily give an accurate account of the historical origin of the atrium, particularly for this part of Italy, which became Roman territory only after the construction of some of the atrium houses standing in 79 CE, but the cultural attitudes they articulate and some of the symbolism they attribute to this space may still be applicable here. The functional character of the atrium in House VI.16.26, which lacks elaborate wall or floor decoration, supports the association of atria with more utilitarian aspects of domestic life as well as with reception of visitors. Similarly, the mixture of cooking and serving vessels, personal effects and clutter refuse in the secondary atrium of the House of the Menander may also reflect such a vision. In fact, it is interesting that out of Allison's whole sample of thirty houses, which together include thirty-five atria, only a minority – thirteen atria – have evidence for wall paintings.

In this case, then, it is our own cultural preconceptions that lead us to see an incompatibility between architecture and movable furnishings which the occupants of the houses would probably not have perceived themselves. But there are also instances requiring a different explanation. In the House of the Ceii, for example, the small room g, which had storage shelves fixed around its walls, was once decorated with wall paintings. These were damaged and obscured by the shelves, implying that what may originally have served as a small decorated living room had subsequently been converted for use as a store. Allison notes a similar instance of this kind of change (which she refers to as 'downgrading') in room i of the same house, where a fixed hearth suggests that the room was used for cooking, while the walls carry paintings. We should not assume a priori that such decoration was inappropriate to a cooking area, but the fact that, out of forty-four rooms with fixed hearths in Allison's sample, only one other example has wall paintings (House VIII.5.9) while the remainder are finished with plain plaster suggests that the combination of hearth and decoration was probably not intentional and that, like room g, it did result from a change in the use of space within the house.[9]

---

[9] In contrast, painted shrines are often associated with cooking areas: Foss 1997.

Seismic damage might have caused the reorganisation of domestic activity, either temporarily while repairs were undertaken, or permanently if parts of the house ceased to be used or the property was no longer considered viable for the needs of the original owners. But the adaptation of domestic space for use in new ways is also an integral part of the process of living, and given that the House of the Ceii was occupied for 200 years, it would perhaps be surprising if evidence for changes in the configuration and use of space were completely absent. Households grow and contract as available resources fluctuate, children are born and leave and partners marry, divorce and die (these patterns are all documented by Bradley for high-status Roman families based on textual evidence: Bradley 1991, 125–176). This domestic life cycle means that changes in the requirements placed on living space are part of a normal process as the architectural structure is reshaped to suit the requirements of new, or newly configured, households. The easiest elements of the domestic environment to adapt to these changing requirements are the movable finds and furniture. Aspects of the architecture, such as the location of doorways, decoration of the walls, and even the boundaries of the house itself, were altered during the lifetime of the houses, as demonstrated particularly by the House of the Menander. But this process would have been much more expensive and disruptive, and is therefore likely to have been relatively slow to catch up with the household's requirements. Such changes are likely, however, to account for the contradictory impression given in rooms g and i in the House of the Ceii by the décor and the fixtures and finds they contained.

The relatively long lifespan of these houses also raises another consideration, which is the need for on-going maintenance. In House VI.16.26 the stack of roof tiles in the atrium seems to indicate that repairs were anticipated or being carried out at the time of the eruption, and the various building materials in the House of the Menander suggest that redecoration was either planned or taking place here, too. It is possible that this work was being undertaken to repair damage caused by earthquakes, but work on the roof to remedy the effects of general wear and tear, and redecoration of rooms, must also have been a normal activity for residents of a building of this age. Some of the works which were being prepared for or were in progress at the time of the destruction might be the result of this kind of routine process. Evidence of the inhabitants thinking ahead to the need for this kind of maintenance can perhaps be seen in the form of three compluvium tiles found in basement room b of the House of the Menander.

CONCLUSIONS: TOWARDS A DYNAMIC AND SOCIALLY INCLUSIVE
MODEL FOR HOUSEHOLDS AT POMPEII

The discussion of the three houses presented above provides a starting point
for building a more complex model for understanding the distribution of
artefacts in ancient domestic contexts and a variety of conclusions emerge
which could be tested against a larger sample of houses. By distinguishing
between items which may have been in use and those more likely to
have been in storage or in refuse deposits, it is possible to explain some
of the variability indicated by the artefact distributions in these houses.
Selective discussion of examples of the three organisational patterns I have
highlighted here shows that all of them contribute in various ways to an
impression of confusion and ambiguity in the archaeological record and
that this is unlikely to have been entirely due to disturbance caused by
seismic activity. Even so, there is only limited spatial separation of objects
and architectural features which are likely to have been used for different
activities. Such a conclusion suggests not only that we cannot answer the
commonly raised question about precise room function, but also that this
is probably not the right question to be asking. Nevertheless, it does not
mean that detailed study of artefacts and their spatial settings is unhelpful.
On the contrary, by thinking in more detail about how our own cultural
perspective affects our interpretation, and about some of the processes
which may have created the archaeological record, it is possible to come to
a better understanding of what multifunctionality and flexibility in spatial
usage may actually have involved in a Roman household.

A major underlying feature of many of the patterns outlined here is
an interplay between activities operating on different timescales. Lin Foxhall has pointed out how in Greek contexts archaeologists have tended
to ignore short-term change which took place over days, weeks, months
or a few years, and think instead on the scale of events taking place over
the medium-term – a period of a generation or several generations (Foxhall 2000, 485). Indeed this timeframe has been seen as the one classical
archaeology is best fitted to investigate (Snodgrass 1991, 69). Yet what we
see in individual houses at Pompeii is the result of both medium-term
and also short-term activities, taking place both in linear and in cyclical
fashion. Rather than aspiring simply to characterise the house as a static
entity frozen in time at the moment of its destruction, paying attention
to these different scales can give us a richer, more dynamic and more
socially inclusive picture. Distinguishing between interlocking timeframes
of short duration is difficult or impossible to do based on the archaeological

evidence alone, but ethnographic parallels and ancient literary sources can assist by suggesting possible interpretations of the archaeological material.

The multifunctional and flexible use of space indicated by patterns of artefact distributions relate to the shortest timescales, and many of the activities they reveal may have been cyclical, with the same tasks ceasing and resuming in a particular location on a regular basis. At the scale of a single day, a formal atrium like that of the House of the Ceii may have seen a variety of activities at different times. Aside from the reception of visitors, members of the household might have come here to draw water, taking toilet articles from the cupboard in the south-east corner of the room to wash, or a cup from the chest in the north-east corner, to drink from. Here, too, tools may have been left as their users came in or out. Different members of the household would have passed through on their way to room i, perhaps to use the latrine, warm themselves by the hearth, or prepare or fetch food. At nightfall, lamps may have been taken from the shelves under the stairs in order to provide some light. On a seasonal basis the pattern might have changed somewhat: on summer evenings the focus of activity might have shifted more towards the rooms at the back of the house to take advantage of breezes around the garden. Meals might have been prepared on a brazier in a room adjoining the garden, and eaten off vessels taken from the shelves of room g.

On a longer timescale, the state of repair of a house must have echoed the fortunes, or the priorities, of its owners, as we see in the case of House VI.16.26. The property contains relatively little decoration, most of it consisting of styles of wall decoration traditionally dated to the second and first centuries BCE. The majority of the rooms, including the atrium, had only plain plaster walls, and in contrast with the Vitruvian model, the emphasis of this space seems to have been on functionality. The southern area around the peristyle may have fallen into disrepair, or even been converted into a separate unit, and work seems to have been under way on the roof. Here, then, was a house which does not seem to have attracted much care and attention from its owners for some considerable time before the eruption, possibly even for several generations if the wall paintings can be used as a guide. (Of course, the owners need not have been the same family throughout this whole period.)

Multigenerational time is seen even more clearly in the House of the Menander, at both small and large scales. On a small scale, in a wealthy household like this one the possessions of one generation may have rep-resented an accumulation of items, some of which may have been passed down through the family, while others may have been acquired at different times by the owners. The silver hoard found in the basement may be an illustration of this process since it consists of vessels made over an extended period between the mid first century BCE and the mid first century CE in different styles and with different designs, and is not a matched service which could have been purchased together. On a larger scale the structure of the house itself also shows the effects of change over time. The evidence for expansion of the property boundaries suggests a gradual increase in the wealth and status of successive generations of owners. The original core, consisting of the atrium and surrounding rooms, was comparable in ground area to the House of the Ceii, although there was also a garden whose size and layout cannot now be determined (Ling 1997, 223–225). In its final form, however, the house covered roughly six times that area. But while the overall trajectory during more than two centuries of occupation is one of dramatic growth, Ling's detailed analysis of the insula's building phases shows that there were periods of contraction. For example, for part of its history the house was also connected with its neighbour to the west, the so-called House of the Smith. The House of the Menander seems to have suffered, losing a room on its north-west corner, when the two were subsequently separated (Ling 1997, 134). Similarly, the provision of a separate stable-court, which may have served to bring large quantities of provisions into the house to supply the household, or may even have been part of a commercial or farming enterprise (as Ling argues: Ling 1997, 252), is an indication of a flourishing household, but there may have been a period of recession immediately before the eruption since the stable-court seems to have fallen out of use by then. While it is impossible to reconstruct the individual domestic circumstances which led either to periods of expansion or to setbacks, such changes are, again, an important reminder of the intimate connection between the physical structure of a building, its contents, and the fortunes of its owners. They also underline the way in which different timescales can offer contradictory information: short-term changes can move in a different direction from longer-term trends.

There is thus a tension between the conclusions to be drawn from the more durable evidence of longer-term behavioural patterns, and the less permanent material representing smaller-scale, shorter-term activities. These two different aspects of the archaeological record are likely to coincide to some extent with the perspectives of different social groups within the household. While the literary sources emphasise, and the architecture creates an appearance of, monumentality, this does not seem to have been the only, or even the main, consideration governing the organisation of the contents of the houses. The presence in the atrium of cupboards containing household implements emphasises alternative uses made of this space by different members of the household. Unlike the monumental architecture which serves as a cue to signal its function as a reception space, these other roles were not, as far as we can see, made permanent in the architecture: aside from built-in shelves and cupboards they can be detected only through the more ephemeral evidence of the finds. The social hierarchy of the household is expressed through the durability of the material correlates for the activities of the different household members, reinforcing the dominance of the *dominus*. It is unclear whether the performance of domestic activities in the atrium was part of the ideological construction of the household as an institution, but this is a possibility. If the view of Augustan culture as manipulating the virtuous elite wife as a public symbol of a man's domestic probity (Milnor 2005, *passim*) can be extended to the Campanian context, one might infer that the presence of domestic equipment in the atrium during the *salutatio* formed part of a single larger rhetorical construction of domestic order.

Another component may have been a view into the atrium at other times of day, with household members visible, busily engaged in domestic chores. This possibility is perhaps supported by the artfulness with which the view of the domestic interior from the street is constructed: as Shelley Hales points out, while appearing to lay the house open to scrutiny, in fact the layout hides the majority of space, including the entrances to most of the rooms (Hales 2003,112 and 119). To date most attention has focused on the way in which the fauces–atrium–tablinum alignment would have displayed the *dominus* to visitors. It would, nevertheless, have been equally possible to create a tableau of domestic industry in the atrium aimed at passers-by, without exposing activity elsewhere in the house to scrutiny; and in fact plaster casts of the main doors of the House of the Ceii show that at the time of the eruption they stood open, presenting such a view (Michel 1990, 18). (Of course, it is impossible to know whether the open doors may have been a response to the events surrounding the eruption, but if Pliny the Younger can be believed that the eruption began in the afternoon, falling debris may have prevented closure of doors which were customarily left open at that time of day.)

The patterns of flexibility and multifunctionality highlighted here show that there is also an additional reading of the evidence, which offers the perspective of the household as a whole, rather than that of the *dominus* alone, and the two perspectives could have co-existed: the arrangement of smaller-scale domestic activities suggests that in addition to keeping up appearances, considerable attention was also given to practical issues such as the availability of space for large storage vessels, keeping things at or close to the places where they were needed, and ways of keeping warm or cool at different times of year. Thus, the comfort and convenience of the household as a whole were an important, integral part of its overall pattern of organisation. Studying the finds, which represent the result of short-term activities by a range of household members including women and slaves, alongside the architecture therefore produces a more deeply textured understanding of the household as a composite social unit with its own logic and agenda, and offers a new perspective which to some extent counterbalances the traditional image of the household as revolving around the requirements of an elite male *dominus*.

CHAPTER 6

Housing as symbol: elite self-presentation in North Africa under Roman rule

The scenery offers much variety, in some places the route is blocked by trees, in others it takes in wide meadows, where large flocks of sheep and herds of cattle . . . thrive in the spring sunshine, and on the fertile grazing. My villa is a convenient size . . . Tell me, now, don't I have good cause for living in, staying at, loving, such a place.

Pliny the Younger, *Letters* 2.17

Considering power dynamics . . . at the scale of the household may yield insights into how . . . certain household members acquired or reproduced social status or economic wealth in the larger context of their community or society.

Hendon 2005, 186

INTRODUCTION

In previous chapters discussion has centred on the way in which the physical remains of ancient houses can be used as a means of exploring some of the social and cultural patterns by which those houses were shaped. In this chapter I shift the focus onto the representation of the domestic sphere, using the material record to look at the way in which a house can play a symbolic role as an expression of the ideas and values of its owner. To do so, I look at housing from North Africa between the second and fifth centuries CE, which is particularly well known for its large numbers of distinctive polychrome mosaic floors. It is these mosaics, and some of the ways in which their iconography seems to have been manipulated by the members of the North African elite to convey a distinctive ideology, which are the subject of this chapter.

One of the best-known mosaics from the region, referred to by modern scholars as the Dominus Julius mosaic (Plate 6.1), provides a starting point for discussion, and detailed consideration of the iconography offers a basis for addressing a range of wider questions about the way in which the elites

Plate 6.1 The Dominus Julius mosaic, from Carthage

of Late Roman North Africa manipulated their domestic environments in order to reinforce their personal status. The mosaic comes from ancient Carthage, the most important Roman city in North Africa, and was probably created between approximately 380 and 400 CE. Now displayed in the Bardo Museum in Tunis, the mosaic was excavated during the early twentieth century in a Roman house. In common with a significant minority of other such floors it is a figurative piece. Its style is characteristically North African: the image is organised in three registers with all of the motifs facing a single direction. It apparently depicts a large house set in a rural landscape which is evoked through a series of vignettes taking the viewer through different seasons of the year. At the centre of the top register a female figure, distinguishable by her long hair and fine robe, sits fanning herself on a bench among cypress trees and is approached by other figures bringing agricultural produce. By her feet is a bird-house, whose occupants scratch at the ground for food. To the viewer's left a man in a short tunic and with short hair brings ducks. Two tiny figures collect olives from a tree, while a woman brings a basket. To the right the image is less well preserved, but it is clear that a further woman brings a lamb. A second, male, figure is only partially preserved, but behind him stands a field of grain. A motif beside it may represent a kennel, since a dog is tied up in front of it. There is a marked contrast between the central woman, who is seated and at leisure, and the other figures, who are moving towards her, bringing produce. This contrast, together with differences in dress, suggests that the seated woman is a member of the elite, while the others are of lower social status – the men wearing the short tunics of agricultural workers of slave or peasant status.

The bottom register contains two separate scenes, but they represent similar scenarios. This time a standing woman with a chair and a rose bush behind her is approached by a partially preserved male figure bearing a basket of roses. On her other side a figure now lost places fish at her feet, while at the same time she receives a necklace or garland from a woman who holds a casket. Behind her, a cat looks on. Separated from this group by a tree there is a second scene, which has fruit trees in the background: to the right a seated male figure dressed in long robes receives a scroll from a standing figure dressed in a shorter tunic. The scroll is visibly addressed *Iu. dom.* and gives the mosaic its modern name. This figure is interpreted as the owner of the estate depicted and also as the householder who originally commissioned the mosaic: Julius. Behind Julius a further male figure, also dressed in a tunic, brings a large basket, apparently containing fruit, and also grasps a rabbit by its back legs. His feet are invisible behind a barrier.

A grape vine curls around one of two trees beside him. Again, a contrast is implied between the elite status of the two figures who are receiving items, and the lower status of those who are presenting the items.

Top and bottom registers echo each other in some respects, and draw the eye towards the seated figures, following the movement of the other individuals. This effect is echoed on the two sides of the central register by images of an elite man on horseback, interpreted as a second image of Julius, paralleling the two elite female figures in the top and bottom registers, which are both interpreted as his wife shown in different contexts. The mounted Julius is followed by an attendant (to his right) and (to his left) two further figures with hunting dogs. But the centrepiece of the whole landscape, stationary in the middle of the central register, is what appears to be an elaborate country house. The exact arrangement of the building the mosaicist was trying to represent has been debated, since the way in which perspective is dealt with is difficult for a modern viewer to understand; but the constituent elements are clear. This is an ashlar masonry structure with a tiled roof, a central entrance and flanking towers. An arcade running between the towers may represent a series of windows or a veranda on an upper storey, or alternatively a colonnaded peristyle at ground level in an interior courtyard. A lone palm tree may indicate a park within the estate (Slim 1995, 141) or fruit trees located in the courtyard. To the rear are further constructions: on analogy with the excavated remains of Roman domestic buildings, three small domes emitting plumes of smoke or steam probably represent a private bath suite, and a larger one alongside may be part of the same complex. A tall, square structure with tiled roof may represent a large reception room with a high ceiling and correspondingly raised roof-line. The building provides a conceptual focus which unifies the different thematic elements of the mosaic as a whole.

As a point of entry into the symbolic role played by elite housing in Roman North Africa, the Dominus Julius mosaic is doubly fascinating, not only because it was laid in a domestic context, but also because it depicts the exterior of a domestic building – a subject which is relatively unusual, not only in surviving mosaics from this and other parts of the Roman Empire, but also in ancient iconography more generally. What might the choice of this subject say about the owner of the house in which it was located? And what can the image as a whole reveal about the meaning and associations which the idea of such a house carried in the North African context? In order to begin to address these questions, it is necessary to situate the mosaic as precisely as possible within its architectural, social and iconographic context.

THE ARCHITECTURAL CONTEXT OF THE DOMINUS JULIUS MOSAIC

Limited information is available about the original architectural setting of the Dominus Julius mosaic. Its French excavator, Alfred Merlin, reported very briefly that it came from a Roman house in the district of Tunis between the hill of Juno and the Byrsa, an area close to the centre of ancient Carthage. Unfortunately no plan of the excavation was published, and nothing is known about the layout of the house from which it came, although Merlin did briefly document the immediate architectural context, which he says was an apsidal space. The apse itself was furnished with a poorly preserved patterned mosaic which does not survive. Around its circumference was a wall enclosing a raised border of mosaic. Merlin suggested the possibility that there may also originally have been a fountain at the centre of the apse, which had been destroyed by a burial found to have been dug into this area at a later date. Nothing was said about any objects associated with the floor which might have suggested how the space was used. Interpretation of the function of the room must therefore rely on comparison between Merlin's description and evidence from other, better-documented, excavations.

The size and shape of the Dominus Julius panel suggest that it originally covered the floor of a large reception room. By the fourth century apsidal reception rooms were a relatively common feature of private houses across the Roman world. Such houses are normally organised around a peristyle courtyard which would have given access to the apsidal room and to other domestic spaces. There is sometimes clear evidence that in the apsidal room itself the apse was designed to hold a stibadium, a curved dining couch. Such couches seem to have varied somewhat in design: in a few excavated examples traces are preserved of a masonry structure on which cushions would presumably have been placed directly. In others the design of the mosaic floor echoes the curving form of a wooden couch. Where neither of these features is present, the use of a stibadium is often inferred on the basis of the apse alone. The recorded measurements of the apse accompanying the Dominus Julius mosaic fall close to the centre of the range known from other examples, and it is likely that the Dominus Julius mosaic itself was also originally located in a room designed to accommodate a stibadium in its rear apse.[1]

---

[1] Merlin described the apse as curving away from the top of the Dominus Julius panel and as slightly narrower, measuring 4.8 m on its straight side, compared with the width of the main panel, which was 5.65 m. The dimensions of surviving stibadia and stibadium mosaics range in size from 3.2 m up to 7.4 m in diameter (Morvillez 1996, 158).

While today the archaeological remains of such rooms look stark and uninviting, they would originally have been richly furnished. Their mosaic floors are likely to have been complemented by colourful wall tapestries and the stibadia themselves would have been provided with embroidered cushions, as textual evidence, images of banquets and fragments of fabrics all suggest (Maguire 2002, 239–240). Merlin's description of the Dominus Julius room can probably be interpreted as indicating that a fountain was located on the back wall above the diners' heads, discharging into a mosaic channel which would have run behind the diners. If he is right also to identify a fountain at the centre of the apse, the water probably flowed from the channel into that fountain, which would have been located at the centre of the stibadium (Figure 6.1). Water features are a frequent element of elite Roman dining spaces from Early to Late Empire. As well as being aesthetically pleasing, fountains and channels like these may have helped to keep the occupants of the couches cool by circulating cold water. Cups and dishes could also have been placed in or beside the stream of water to chill food and drink (for Roman Italy, see Pliny the Younger, *Letters* 5.6.37 with Richardson 1988). Such devices would have been particularly welcome in the hot, dry African summer, and indeed in this region there are numerous surviving examples of Roman houses with water features located in niches in dining rooms or, more frequently, immediately outside in the courtyard (see Ghiotto 2003).

How many diners would have eaten together in the Dominus Julius room? The probable arrangement of the furniture can be clarified by looking at the stibadium design on a sixth-century mosaic from a square room in the so-called villa of the Falconer at Argos (Greece). Here, the curving outline of a couch in the floor mosaic is subdivided into seven segments (Åkerström-Hougen 1974, 34–36, 40, 101–117). Traditionally, rooms were frequently configured to accommodate seven couches, so it seems likely that these represent individual cushions or couches. The Dominus Julius dining room, where the apse has similar dimensions, may have accommodated a comparable number.[2] The diners' situation within the curving alcove would have given them an excellent view of the main part of the room. Textual sources suggest that banquets may have incorporated entertainments by performers such as acrobats (Jones 1991), and this main part of

---

[2] The stibadium outline on the Argos mosaic measures 4.6 m in diameter and is therefore only slightly smaller than the recorded dimensions of the apse in the Dominus Julius mosaic which was 4.8 m across, although the number of diners might also have depended to some extent on the depth of the apse, which is not noted in Merlin's description.

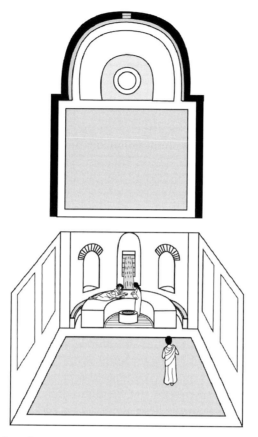

Figure 6.1 Hypothetical reconstruction of the architectural setting for the Dominus Julius mosaic: plan (top) and three-dimensional artist's impression (below). Shading indicates mosaics noted by Merlin

the room is presumably where they would have been staged. Slaves and servants must also have used this space in the course of fetching and carrying the dishes and plates, and performing other tasks required of them.

The functional division between the apse and the principal space was accentuated by the design of the mosaic, which contrasted the figured scene in the main room with the patterned panel in the adjoining apse. As Merlin's description makes clear, the design on the main part of the floor was oriented so that it would have maximum impact on those entering the room or viewing it from the doorway. Once the diners had taken their places on the couch, the images would have appeared upside-down. This may partly have been because, at over 25 square metres in area, the scale of the panel made it difficult to take in the whole design from a single location. Today the Bardo Museum displays the mosaic on a wall, giving visitors a panorama of the whole image. In its original location the ancient viewer would have had to move across the floor, looking at the individual vignettes in order to get a mental picture of the entire piece. The mosaic was therefore perhaps best observed en route to the apse while he or she was still taking in the room, rather than upon leaving, when the space as a whole may have become more familiar and the mosaic itself might have attracted less attention. The orientation may also have been intended to be particularly effective in certain social situations: reception of guests in the Roman world in general was a somewhat theatrical activity, and the textual descriptions and artistic depictions of dinner parties, together with surviving evidence about their architectural settings, all suggest that a banquet was also a spectacle. The decoration of the dining room might therefore have been arranged partly in order to complement the tableau of the diners, framed within the rear apse with the fountain behind them.

Apart from dining, it is unclear what activities may have taken place in apsidal rooms like this one. Similar spaces occur in country villas of this period elsewhere in the Empire, albeit on a larger scale, and these have been interpreted as multifunctional, fulfilling a range of roles including that of reception hall and setting for business dealings (Rossiter 1991, 202). This kind of more generalised role may also be applicable in the urban context, to rooms like that of the Dominus Julius mosaic. As well as entertaining his social equals here, the *dominus* perhaps received visitors of lower social status who came to pay their respects or ask for favours, in a manner comparable to the *salutatio* mentioned in Chapter 5. By the late fourth century when the Dominus Julius mosaic was created, the space associated with the *salutatio* at Pompeii, the atrium, was no longer a regular component of elite houses, yet textual sources suggest that the *salutatio* itself, or something like it, was a still part of socio-political life both in Italy and in the provinces. (The Dominus Julius mosaic itself could even be construed as a rustic version of this practice, with master and mistress receiving tributes from visitors.) The apse would have made a striking location from which the *dominus* could receive such callers, framed by the architecture: as in the earlier tablinum, the conceptual separation between this and the main part of the room would have focused attention on him and created a barrier between him and the rest of the room, accentuating the gulf between visitor and visited which was already emphasised by the sheer lavishness of the architecture.

Used in this way, the apsidal room may ultimately have held resonances of the apses and domes of the palaces where the Emperor received his subjects, the architectural language of Imperial power being adopted and adapted further down the social hierarchy until it reached the provincial urban *domus*. As in the Imperial case, the apse itself recalled the public architecture of the basilica (where the magistrate presided) and may also have had faintly cultic or religious connotations. These associations may have been appropriated by the *dominus* to whom this Carthaginian house belonged, in order to emphasise his own more localised position of authority and status. Sadly, nothing is known about the remainder of that house, although given the size and expense of the mosaic it is likely that this was one of several richly decorated reception rooms the owner had at his disposal for entertaining guests and receiving callers (compare Ellis 1991, 120).

The Dominus Julius mosaic was thus part of a larger architectural ensemble which worked together with the floor to create an atmosphere of opulence and to distance the occupants of the apse from anyone in the remainder of the room. The sight of the householder framed within the apse may also have conjured up associations with public architecture and perhaps even with the emperor. But to what extent is it possible to be more specific about what was being communicated to the different audiences who may have viewed it? And what can we learn about the significance attached to the central house motif? In order to explore these questions it is necessary to look more closely at the iconography of the Dominus Julius mosaic itself.

INTERPRETING THE ICONOGRAPHY OF THE DOMINUS JULIUS MOSAIC

Although mosaicists probably made some use of pattern-books as part of the creative process, no parallels have been excavated for the way in which the Dominus Julius mosaic depicts a rural building in a populated landscape. Indeed in this respect the mosaic is part of a trend seen from the end of the second century CE onwards, when the North African provinces witnessed the appearance of a variety of images which seem to be unique. This departure from the stock scenes used more commonly has been taken to imply that patrons were closely involved in choosing particular designs and that they asked for special motifs which were not part of the usual repertoire (Dunbabin 1978, 24–26).

A related desire to 'personalise' images in some way is found in mosaics throughout the geographical and chronological extent of the Roman Empire and may also suggest active involvement of the householder in determining the choice of subject (Dunbabin 1999, 317–324). A clear example comes from a house in Pompeii where the black and white mosaic on the floor of an atrium depicts shipping containers of a shape normally used for *garum* (fish sauce). These are shown as carefully labelled with the name of Umbricius Scaurus, known from epigraphic evidence as a *garum* merchant. Scaurus is assumed to have owned the property at one time and to have commissioned the mosaic in question (Curtis 1984). The rather more subtle inclusion of the scroll marked *Iu. dom.* on the Dominus Julius mosaic can perhaps be explained in the same way. Text is also sometimes used to personalise more generic scenes by adding names, for example to animals, as in a threshold panel dating to the later third or fourth century from a house in Oudna, south of Carthage, depicting a hunt with two dogs whose names are spelled out as 'Ederatus' ('ivy-patterned') and 'Mustela' ('weasel'). It is, of course, unclear whether the patron of the floor ever owned a hunting dog named Ederatus, and some of the floors may be the product of imagination or wishful thinking, but this does not undermine the suggestion that the choice of subject matter suggests active involvement of a patron.

While the Dominus Julius mosaic itself is unique, the individual iconographic elements of the piece have associations with other surviving images as well as with themes occurring in other visual media and in literature. Those associations extend not only to the immediate area of the site and the North African provinces more widely, but also to the rest of the Roman world beyond, drawing the mosaics, and by extension also their owners, into a larger cultural *koine* (community). By exploring some of the associations of these elements, it is possible to work towards a more detailed understanding of the meaning the mosaic may have communicated, and of the symbolic value and associations of the central house image.

The basic agricultural theme is one which recurs in African mosaics from the first century CE onwards. For example, a series of partially preserved emblemata from the floor of a room in a coastal villa at Zliten in Tripolitania (modern Libya) dates perhaps to the late first century. The two better-preserved panels show men and women cultivating crops by hand, threshing with horses and cattle, and tending to goats (Dunbabin 1978, Plate xxxvi, 95 and 96). A floor from a house at Oudna, which is dated to approximately 160–180 or 200–220 CE, carries similar scenes of rural labour

Plate 6.2 Mosaic floor from Oudna

but hunting is added and the arrangement is rather different (Plate 6.2). Its series of vignettes are seemingly part of a single landscape, although they are to some extent disconnected by their arrangement. The centre and end of the floor to the viewer's right are occupied by the ploughmen and goatherd, the front edge and left-hand end show hunters. To the front left a figure disguised in a goat skin traps partridges in a net by stealth. On the left-hand end a group of mounted huntsmen have speared a big cat, while to the right front two figures on foot finish off a boar with the assistance of two hunting dogs.

The produce shown on the Dominus Julius mosaic is generally interpreted as symbolising the fertility and fruitfulness of the landscape surrounding the central house. Nevertheless, on closer inspection additional points emerge. In this, and indeed all the North African mosaics in which crops and livestock are depicted, there is little about the produce which marks it out as specifically African in character (Nevett 2008). Where particular species are identifiable they include crops such as grapes, apples and roses; animals such as sheep, goats, horses and cattle; and game such as duck and rabbit or hare. All are found widely around the Mediterranean including in Italy itself. Local species did undoubtedly play a role in agriculture in some areas of Roman Africa, particularly in Tripolitania where conditions were more arid: for instance, camels were probably used for ploughing (Shaw 1995 [1979], 698), and camel meat also occasionally seems to have been eaten (van der Veen *et al.* 1996, 242). But while the camel, in particular, seems to have been something of a prized possession in the Tripolitanian interior where it features prominently on rock-cut funerary reliefs in a variety of roles (Shaw 1995 [1979], 718–719), that prestige does not seem to have earned it a place in the agricultural mosaics, even in Tripolitania itself.

Environmental samples (evidence for the remains of flora and fauna) from various regions of North Africa provide a another perspective on the iconography. Faunal evidence from a range of excavations in and around ancient Carthage itself, reviewed by Michael Mackinnon (Mackinnon, forthcoming), shows that the main sources of meat were (in descending order of importance) domesticated sheep and goats, pigs and cattle. At the same time the proportion of game animals such as deer, hare and rabbit, and wild birds, was small, suggesting that such animals were raised in the area around the city to cater for an urban elite. Further afield, samples from Tripolitania show a predominance of the same domesticated species, and indicate that in that region, as well as birds and rabbits, game animals also included local species such as porcupine, gazelle and antelope, although here again game represented only a very small proportion of the diet (van der Veen *et al.* 1996, 242, 258). Poultry also played only a minor role compared with other meat sources (Barker 1979, 11–12), and meat formed only a relatively small proportion of the overall diet (van der Veen *et al.* 1996, 259).

In sum, in treating agricultural themes the African mosaicists chose not to represent any characteristic local flora and fauna and also emphasised prestige produce at the expense of staples, giving disproportionate attention to animals rather than crops, and to game in relation to domesticated species. Such selectivity is an indication that, contrary to what is often assumed, the images cannot be taken as literal representations of the countryside and farming regimes of these provinces. Instead they should be seen as a claim by wealthy householders to have access to the same expensive, prestigious foods as elites elsewhere in the Roman world. At the same time they also draw on the popular Hellenistic and Roman elite discourse, seen in a variety of media, in which rural life was idealised (compare Shaw 1995 [1979], 697).

Salvatore Aurigemma, excavator of the Zliten mosaic, suggested that the individual panels of that particular floor were intended as allegories of different months, their cycle being indicated by various agricultural tasks which are appropriate to different times of the farming year. The passage of the seasons is a major theme of North African mosaics over a long period, from the second century through to the fifth or even the sixth century CE, and it is also found in mosaics from other Roman provinces, including Britain. The same idea has frequently also been viewed as integral to the Dominus Julius floor, the roses and grapes of the bottom register representing spring and autumn respectively, while the olive harvest and grain of the upper register evoke first winter, then summer. As far as we know, this floor is unique in the way that the seasonal tasks are integrated as part of a wider landscape rather than being placed in separate panels or emblemata. The evocation of the seasons does, nevertheless, tie the floor into a wider sphere of art and ideas, linking it not only with other parts of Roman Africa, but also with the Empire beyond.

Another element of the activity depicted on the Dominus Julius mosaic which connects it with a wider thematic group is the hunt motif alluded to in the central register by the mounted aristocrat and the men with dogs. Hunting of dangerous animals such as lions and boars is frequently represented as an aristocratic pursuit in Graeco-Roman culture, and the theme became particularly popular in North Africa in the later second century, continuing into the fifth century CE. Such images expressed the elevated status of the owners of the mosaics by implying their participation in the elite pastime of hunting. The inclusion of the hunt theme in the Dominus Julius mosaic can thus be viewed both as an expression of elite social standing and, like the allusion to the theme of the seasons, as a claim to membership in a wider cultural *koine*.

The dominus Julius image is unique among the surviving North African agricultural mosaics in giving such prominence to the figure of the *dominus* himself as a focus for the activities of the surrounding figures. While the representation of both aristocratic figures and workers together on the Oudna floor, for example, parallels the Dominus Julius mosaic, its emphasis is different: rather than being the centre of the viewer's attention and the workers' activities, in the earlier image the horsemen are simply a part of the rural landscape, like the workers themselves. Nevertheless, comparanda can be suggested for the way in which the mosaicist of the Dominus Julius floor indicated a hierarchical pattern of social relationships, showing the lower-status figures bringing produce intended for Julius and for his wife.

These link the image, not so much with other domestic or private contexts, but with the iconography used on public monuments. In the earlier Roman period the theme appears on triumphal arches such as that of the emperor Titus in the city of Rome itself, where reliefs showing the procession of captives carrying booty were a graphic representation of the power of the conquering emperors and part of a wider iconographic repertoire. The motif came into its own in the later Roman period where it received much greater emphasis, featuring on a variety of state monuments and also in private contexts in other media including wall painting and metal work.[3] The use of this iconography in the Dominus Julius mosaic is therefore part of a wider trend towards the adoption of the Imperial language of self-presentation as a mark of elite status and reinforces the effect of the floor's architectural setting.

Having explored the iconography of various elements of the Dominus Julius mosaic, the final crucial aspect to look at is the central motif, the house itself. Again, the theme of the villa in a rural setting is not new and the idea can be seen in earlier images from Roman Italy: representations of landscapes containing elaborate country and seaside houses are an integral element of Roman wall paintings from the later first century BCE and first century CE. In these images the villa is often simply one element of a wider landscape, although it is also sometimes shown in isolation, framed as if on display in a gallery. In either case the architecture represented seems to be fantastic rather than representing a building which actually existed. Nonetheless, numerous examples of luxurious Roman houses of this date have been found in the countryside of southern Italy in a variety of locations including just outside the walls of towns such as Pompeii, on coastal hillsides overlooking the sea, and also on hills further inland. Texts such as Pliny the Younger's discussion of his Laurentian villa (*Letters* 2.17, quoted at the start of this chapter) also attest the importance of the idea of a country retreat in the minds of the Roman elite of the same period. Thus, while the villas depicted in the wall paintings are not literal representations of structures seen by the artists, they do seem to have been stimulated by an emphasis on country houses in elite culture, and they had a symbolic significance (compare Wallace-Hadrill 1998).

In the North African provinces rural buildings are occasionally represented in preserved wall paintings: for example, a cryptoporticus (covered

---

[3] See Ploumis 1997, who also points out that the idea can also be detected in early Christian imagery in scenes of the adoration of the infant Christ.

Plate 6.3 Mosaic showing square and round buildings from a Nilotic scene, from El Alia

walkway) dating to the first century CE in the seaside villa at Zliten in Tripolitania mentioned above included images on its vault of a dispersed group of two-storey houses by the seashore. In comparison with the villa paintings from Campania the buildings portrayed are small and simple in character (Aurigemma 1962, 41–69). Structures of a similar scale and form are represented in second-century mosaics, including those from Zliten itself, although in that instance the structures have flat roofs (Aurigemma 1926, 84–97). Rural buildings in the Oudna agricultural mosaic are closer to the Dominus Julius building, featuring pitched roofs (Plate 6.2). More elaborate buildings appear elsewhere: for example, two mosaics from a coastal villa at El Alia depict a river (possibly intended to be the Nile) with a surrounding landscape of animals, people and structures (Gauckler 1910, 39–41) (Plate 6.3). The images draw a striking contrast between various colonnaded buildings with pitched, tiled roofs in Graeco-Roman fashion, and a number of conical structures which are possibly intended to represent indigenous dwellings. (It is unclear, however, whether they bore any resemblance to real dwellings either in the area near the villa or indeed in Egypt.) Like the structures from the Campanian wall paintings, the North African examples are generally interpreted as fantasy buildings, created by the painters and mosaicists as part of the overall composition of an imaginary landscape. The fact that the images sometimes appear sketchy and lacking in detail perhaps contributes to the impression that they are not intended to represent actual buildings.

By the fourth to sixth centuries CE, more elaborate country villa structures can be identified in a small number of mosaic floors, and these have been interpreted as realistic representations of a new building type. In some of the hunting scenes of this date buildings are shown in the distance. A simultaneous narrative technique is sometimes employed in which

Plate 6.4 Part of a mosaic showing a hunt, from Khereddine, near Carthage

different stages of the hunt are depicted in a single scene comprising not only the chase and/or the kill, but also the party setting out. A late fourth- or early fifth-century example from a house in the Khereddine area of Carthage (Plate 6.4) appears to show not only the hunt and an accompanying sacrifice to the goddess Artemis (the latter not shown here) but also the departure from a fortified country house (top left). This is a very different building from those featured on the earlier mosaics: tall and thin with no sign of decoration or luxurious elements like baths, although it does contain the ashlar construction, tiled roof and upper-storey windows. Some of these elements are similar to the house shown in the Dominus Julius mosaic, but the closest parallel for that building belongs to the end of the fourth or early fifth century and is from a triconch (a room with three apses arranged in clover-leaf shape) from the town of Tabarka in modern Tunisia (Gauckler 1910, 303–305; Dunbabin 1978, 271–272).

Like the Dominus Julius mosaic, this floor was excavated early in the twentieth century, and little is known about its architectural context although it is likely to come from a private house. The central part of the floor, which showed a hunt scene, was badly damaged, and the best-preserved sections of the mosaic belong to the apses (Plate 6.5). Each one carried an image of a different rural building, and it seems that these should

(a)

(b)

Plate 6.5 Mosaic panels showing rural buildings, from Tabarka
(a) Panel from the central apse (b) Panel from a side apse (c) Panel from a side apse

(c)

Plate 6.5 (*cont.*)

be taken together with the scene on the main floor as representing part of a single landscape. The buildings are all long and low in shape, occupying most of the available space, but their rural setting is indicated by various agricultural motifs similar to those shown on the Dominus Julius mosaic, including game birds, and on the two subsidiary panels vines trained on circular supports alongside fruit trees. One human figure, a shepherdess, spins while tending her flock. Her scale and location suggest that she is an extension of the agricultural theme and is not intended to distract attention from the building at the centre of the scene.

One panel of the Tabarka mosaic (Plate 6.5a) is wider than the others and was originally laid in the central apse, on axis with the remainder of the room.[4] The focus of interest is a building which provides a closer parallel to that shown on the Dominus Julius mosaic. A number of comparable architectural features are represented including pitched tiled roofs; a large arched entrance; and square corner towers with a series of arcades running between them. Here, too, it is unclear whether the arcades are supposed to be at ground level or in an upper storey. A series of domes running across the front of the complex may represent a granary or a bath house – the latter suggestion paralleling the interpretation of the Dominus Julius mosaic. The section of the building with its own entrance, located at the left-hand end of the Tabarka villa, may also be comparable to the separate tall structure represented on the Dominus Julius mosaic and perhaps indicates some kind of banqueting- or audience-hall. Roses, fruit trees and game birds surrounding the Tabarka structure convey a rural setting, linking it with the other two panels of the same floor. At the bottom left, poorly preserved, a stream perhaps reinforces the idea of fertility and abundance, providing water for agriculture and a home for water fowl.

The Tabarka panels thus play with many of the same ideas and motifs as the Dominus Julius mosaic, but there is a crucial difference: while the villa and grounds of the Dominus Julius mosaic provide a framework within which the status and social relationships of Julius are set out in graphic form, in the Tabarka images the buildings, and the landscape around them, are themselves the focus of interest, and, aside from the solitary shepherdess, the landscape of the estate is an empty one. Thus, despite similarities between the main building depicted in the Tabarka mosaic and the house shown in the Dominus Julius mosaic, the main emphasis of each one is different, and, as outlined above, the Dominus Julius mosaic seems to represent a more complex combination of ideas and symbols.

Unlike the earlier representations, the Dominus Julius and Tabarka mosaics have frequently been taken to offer a life-like picture of a late Roman North African villa (for example Ennaïfer 1996). Nevertheless, as we have just seen, the landscapes depicted in such scenes are selective in what is portrayed, and there are iconographic precedents and parallels for all of the other elements of the scene, including the landscape, the theme of seasonality, the bringing of produce and the hunt, indicating that their significance may be read as symbolic. This suggests that in all probability the building itself is represented in a similarly selective and imaginative manner and is designed to include elements and details which are also symbolic. In fact, despite increasing amounts of archaeological survey in the North African provinces, there have been only a few finds of large country houses with comfortable living accommodation which include facilities such as bath suites. Such finds as these are limited to the area of modern Tunisia and certainly cannot be taken as representative of the North African provinces as a whole (see Nevett 2008). Instead, they raise a range of interesting questions about the meaning of the Dominus Julius building as a visual motif.

The urban context of the house in which the Dominus Julius mosaic originally lay represents an interesting contrast with the rural setting of the villa depicted on it, which is perhaps intended to imply that the owner had rural property in addition to his town house. This pattern of property ownership is seen at an earlier period in Italy itself in texts such as the letters of the first century BCE writers Pliny the Younger and Cicero. For these authors it was important for a man of high social status to supplement his house in the city by owning country estates with comfortable villas which could be used as retreats from the bustle of urban life. Certainly, the value of spending time in the country is echoed at about the time of the mosaic itself by the Christian writer Synesius, who was Bishop at Ptolemais in Cyrenaica between *c.* 390 and 415 CE: some of his surviving *Letters* seem to have been written from estates near Cyrene which he owned or visited (Goodchild 1986, 252–253). The various texts and the mosaic image also allude more indirectly to a long Graeco-Roman bucolic tradition in which the joys of the countryside are idealised (Synesius himself refers to the *Idylls* of Theocritus, a Hellenistic poet from Sicily writing at Alexandria in this tradition: Synesius, *Letters* 114). As with the other aspects of the iconography already discussed, the inclusion of the country house in the image is therefore likely to have been a statement of ideology which was designed to associate its owner with a group of core values and life-style common to the Imperial elite across the different provinces.

The estates of Synesius and his contemporaries have not been identified, but the remains of rural houses of this period from the area around Cyrene suggest that the type of building involved would have been a 'fortified homestead, a building in which comfort was sacrificed to defensibility' (Goodchild 1986, 253). In fact, although the localised environments and settlement histories of the North African countryside are very diverse, archaeological surveys carried out in the provinces of Zeugitana, Byzacena and Tripolitania have tended to find evidence of productive installations (for amphorae and olive oil) and fortified farmsteads, with little mention of the kinds of elegant villa sites found in many other areas of the Roman world. Unsurprisingly, therefore, although the Dominus Julius mosaic is sometimes invoked as evidence of elite rural villas, no building is known which exactly parallels the structure shown either in construction methods or in the range of architectural elements depicted (Nevett 2008). As shown above, the other motifs are selective in what they choose to portray; they also make use of a visual symbolism firmly rooted in the public art of the emperor; and they invoke a network of allusions to long-lived Graeco-Roman aristocratic themes taken from a variety of media. It would perhaps therefore be surprising if the image of the rural villa itself were not shown in a manner which is similarly selective and allusive. So, rather than trying to find buildings on the ground which look like this, it is more helpful to ask what we can learn from the way in which the building is represented, and from the specific characteristics the mosaicist has chosen to emphasise in his representation.

The task of understanding the image of the villa is made more difficult by the fact that to the modern eye it is unclear how the mosaicist is dealing with perspective. Most interpretations have assumed that the arcade running across the front is part of an upper storey, although it has alternatively been understood as showing an internal peristyle behind a front wall (Duval 1986). It is clear that, wherever the craftsman imagined the arcade to be located, he saw it as one of the most important features of the building, since it is picked out in white. It was perhaps selected as an indication of decoration lying inside what otherwise appears as a rather stark, functional building. The idea that it may have provided a comfortable, or even luxurious, living environment is reinforced by the bath house depicted behind, and perhaps also by the structure shown alongside it, if this is correctly interpreted as a reception hall. Other features emphasised include the two square corner towers and the massive, reinforced door at the centre. The impression of a defensible structure this creates is supported by the impression of permanence and solidity conveyed by the outlines of the individual ashlar blocks making up the walls and by the tiled roofs of the two towers.

The variety of features the mosaicist picks out in this image is remarkably close to those shown on the building in the main apse of the Tabarka floor, although those features are not put together in the same manner (or, perhaps, the two structures are envisaged as viewed from different angles). Interpreting the Tabarka building as having an internal peristyle appears particularly convincing as it seems to show a ground level in front of the arcade, and the proportions are wider and shorter. On the Tabarka building details are also rendered in a less delicate, heavier manner: for example, the square windows have thick mullions. The contrasting styles and viewpoints of the two images suggest that the craftsmen who produced them were not working from a single pattern, but that both had remarkably similar ideas about what features it was important to include, features which together communicated similar ideas about the permanence, defensibility and comfort of the building. The central position of the Dominus Julius building in the mosaic as a whole perhaps conveyed related ideas about the power and centrality of the structure in relation to the surrounding landscape. It is interesting that it is this, rather than the figure of Julius (presumably its owner), which takes centre stage. Perhaps there is a sense in which the building symbolises the family and its continuity, which runs beyond the span of any single individual or generation. If so, this would again tie the image in with the ideals of Italian aristocrats of the Early Empire, and reinforce the symbolic, rather than realistic, character of both the villa image, and the mosaic as a whole. Thus, in common with the hunting dogs discussed at the beginning of this section, having such a house depicted on his floor does not necessarily mean that the Carthaginian householder who commissioned this piece actually owned one, merely that he aspired to the values that such a house was seen to represent.

CONCLUSION: ELITE HOUSING AND ITS SYMBOLISM IN LATE
ROMAN NORTH AFRICA

A single mosaic like the Dominus Julius floor is obviously insufficient evidence from which to draw generalised conclusions about the use of domestic decoration in North Africa during the Late Roman period. Nevertheless, by looking in detail at the iconography, and recontextualising the piece as far as possible within its architectural setting and cultural milieu, it is possible to observe at close hand the potential the images used in domestic contexts during this period had as media for communication, and also to understand some of the mechanisms through which such communication took place. We cannot know how many of the users of the room in which the mosaic originally lay would have taken the time to observe the floor closely: the answer perhaps varied according to gender and social status, whether the viewer was seeing the floor for the first time, whether he or she was a resident in the house, the nature of the occasion which brought him or her into the room, the favourability of the lighting conditions, and a host of other variables. Likewise, the observer's consciousness of the kind of nuances of meaning highlighted here must have depended on other factors such as his or her educational and cultural background, and age. Nevertheless, there is a fair amount of overlap or redundancy in the way in which both the architectural setting and various elements of the mosaic project similar or related meanings.

The overriding impression that both the setting and the image create is of the wealth, power and status of the house's owner and his wife. This would have been projected by the architecture of the room, which would have framed anyone sitting within the apse, separated from the main part of the room. At the same time, within the mosaic it is suggested through the two images of Julius – seated and well-dressed, to be served by others, and on horseback. Julius' wife, too, receives gifts in a comparable manner and is shown as leading a leisurely life rather than working. The same idea is reinforced in a number of other ways, through the abundance of the produce and the prominence of luxury items. The activities of the estate workers also reinforce the couple's social and economic position. The fact that the workers treat Julius and his wife in the same way as the emperor is treated in public images is given prominence through repetition, and also conveys status and power relations.

Underlying these ideas, and perhaps not so obvious to the less well-educated viewer, is the demonstration of Julius' participation in a cultural community which stretches beyond Carthage and North Africa, to Roman Italy and the other provinces, which is communicated by drawing on traditional interests of the Graeco-Roman elite in the countryside and in hunting. Above all, however, it is the house itself which carries the most weight, through its centrality in the image, its scale, and the fact that it is static, in contrast with the busy vignettes surrounding it. The building seems to encapsulate all of these ideas: its defensibility standing for power; its decoration and comfort indicating wealth; its reception room emphasising social status; and, finally, its ashlar, tile and baths symbolising its essentially elite, culturally Roman character. At the same time the individual details of the mosaic suggest that *domus* and *dominus* were closely related conceptually in such a way that the house could more literally 'represent' its owner, standing as a symbol for the *dominus* and for the qualities to which his family aspires (even if in reality they have not attained them). Its use in this way underlines conclusions which have been drawn about elite housing across the Roman Empire and over a long period from the Late Republic through to the Late Empire.

Epilogue: domestic space and social organisation in Classical Antiquity

> From ancient times the house has been understood as a microcosmos.
>
> Norberg-Schultz 1985, 91

The preceding chapters highlight the broad spectrum of different scales which can be explored from a domestic perspective, ranging from the intra-household level such as the topic of the Classical Greek symposium or the relative (in)visibility of women and slaves at Pompeii, up to issues spanning whole communities or even regions, such as the self-presentation of elites in late Roman Africa, interaction between cultures in early Roman Delos, or the development of polis society in Early Iron Age Greece. Juxtaposing these different sets of issues and evidence highlights a number of recurrent themes and offers insights, both about the societies discussed and about the strengths and weaknesses of domestic material as a source of information on ancient social life more generally.

The character of houses as buildings clearly varies considerably through space and time within the ancient world, but there are some parallels between the different case studies considered here. Activities prominently represented in the archaeological record are the storage, preparation and consumption of food and drink. Relevant evidence comes from all the locations and periods where finds have been recorded since the most numerous objects preserved tend to be pottery vessels, the majority of which were used for these purposes. In Early Iron Age Greece, in houses where household space was even minimally subdivided, one of the primary, archaeologically visible, functional distinctions drawn was between living areas and those used for food storage. For instance, in some cases at Zagora, when the houses were expanded, rear storage rooms were created and the hearth and living areas moved to newly built spaces. But in later contexts the architecture also attests the significance sometimes accorded to the acts of eating and drinking in Classical Greece, Roman Pompeii or late Roman Carthage, with the provision of decorated rooms furnished with couches on which drinkers or diners could recline. Reception of guests at such occasions seems to have been understood as an important role of elite houses, and architectural elaboration of the rooms where such occasions were probably held was one means of making a good impression on visitors. At Delos and Pompeii decoration is widespread through the house, and more lavish and expensive than in Classical Greece. Instead of a single andron there were a variety of decorated rooms and simple bands of colour on the walls were replaced by detailed painted scenes. On the floors, mosaic designs also became increasingly complex. Sculpture began to be included as part of the overall decorative scheme. These changes are one element of a progressive increase through time in the overall resources spent on elite housing which is also visible in the scale of individual properties and is likely to correspond with growth through time in the economic resources available. (Ian Morris has recently argued that housing, among other evidence, points to marked economic growth in the Greek world: Morris 2005.)

Symposia and banquets are both likely to have been important contexts in which individuals asserted their membership of groups by participating with others. The same occasions would also have established and reconfirmed social hierarchies through seating plans and other non-verbal cues. The significance of these events therefore went beyond the individual households in which they took place because they facilitated social interaction in the context of the community as a whole. The manner in which this relationship between the 'public' and 'private' spheres was conceptualised was not constant through time and space, however. In modern western culture the word 'private' has very particular associations which are not readily applicable to other societies. But if we understand it broadly as expressing how freely individuals and households related to each other and to the wider community, our various case studies suggest a range of different interpretations. The predominance of single-room houses in Early Iron Age Greece offers little sign of any widespread desire to separate individuals or groups from each other. At the same time the use of open porches and exterior work spaces suggests a high degree of integration with the community at large. This is in contrast with the houses of Classical Greece where the andron, complete with anteroom and closable door, offers the possibility of isolating visitors from anyone else in the house; and the andron is just one of a number of different rooms which could have separated the occupants of these houses. This internal segmentation is paired with a restriction on access to the house itself, which was normally confined to a single street door positioned at the end of a narrow corridor and out of sight of the main part of the house, suggesting that only limited and controlled interaction took place with the community outside. The Classical evidence therefore implies a concept of 'privacy' which operated at a series of levels, structuring relationships between individuals within households and relationships between households and the wider world. Whether the ideals materialised in the domestic architecture were actually followed in daily social practice is, of course, impossible to judge: the architecture could be viewed as a statement that a household conformed to socially and culturally accepted norms while those norms could in practice have been subverted to varying degrees.

The evidence of the Campanian atrium-style houses famously suggests a rather different concept of the relationship between household and community. Its large and lavish interior reception spaces support the literary descriptions of visitors entering the house, sometimes in large numbers, for a variety of purposes including for business and political gatherings as well as for social occasions at the invitation of the householder. Here we are dealing with a virtual inversion of the Classical Greek pattern, with both the gaze and the physical presence of outsiders apparently drawn into the interior of the house. Nonetheless, the architecture offers the possibility of controlling both physical and visual access by the construction of narrow corridors, closable doors and partitions. Again, it is not possible to judge to what extent the ideal of openness which such houses seem to embody was actually put into practice on a daily basis. What the evidence does seem to indicate, though, is a radically different concept of the relationship between the occupants of the house and the wider community from that sketched above for the Classical Greek context. While in the latter case the exterior walls constitute a formidable boundary to social interaction, in the Campanian houses the ideal being expressed seems to have been one of permeability.

How uniform these conceptions of the relationship between individuals, households and the wider community were in any one cultural context is impossible to judge, particularly without looking systematically at larger samples of Classical Greek and Campanian structures than those examined here. But the diversity of house-forms in Early Iron Age Greece shows that differing ideas about the necessity of separating individuals within the domestic sphere can co-exist. At the same time the evidence from Delos demonstrates the potential fluidity of the relationship between household and community. Overall, then, while some notion of 'privacy' can be detected through the architecture of the houses discussed in the various chapters, this was constituted rather differently in the different cultural contexts. Furthermore, the fact that contrasting definitions could be present, even within a single community, suggests that the concept of 'privacy' could be flexible and open to negotiation and redefinition.

Organising space so that it conveys adherence to a particular set of cultural ideas about privacy can be seen as just one of a variety of ways in which identity was expressed through housing. Today we are likely to be missing many of the original cues, both because we cannot pick up and interpret every cultural nuance and also simply because of the partial preservation and recording of the original structures. But we can detect and begin to understand enough to show how complex a phenomenon the encoding of identity within the domestic sphere was in Antiquity – just as it is in a modern community. In Classical Greek contexts possession of an andron which provided a space where the male householder and his guests could socialise away from other members of the household can perhaps be viewed as a material expression of citizenship, since such a separation would have implied the safeguarding of the women of the family and hence ensured the parentage of male heirs, preserving the integrity of the citizen body as a whole. While comfortable, however, decoration was modest and the rooms in different houses were very similar to each other, planned on a human scale and clearly intended to accommodate relatively small numbers of people. On a grander scale the Dominus Julius mosaic can also be seen as expressing membership of a group, this time the larger and more widespread community of the elite of the Roman Empire, by drawing on a common repertoire of images and evoking shared ideas. In the houses of Delos, by contrast, the multiplicity of decorated rooms, their lavish decoration and the different spatial configurations seem to say something quite different: alongside participation in a community, there also seems to be an effort to stand out in terms of wealth and the amenities wealth could provide. Hence the (so far as we know) unique character of Cleopatra's statue group and its location facing the street door.

These are just a selection of ways in which aspects of identity might potentially be inferred from some of the material discussed in the case studies. Such inferences need to be made with care, however. As the images of Cleopatra and Dioscorides show, identity is multifaceted and heavily dependent on context. We might deduce from the inscription on the Cleopatra monument, for instance, that the couple are, in modern terms, 'locals' – they are Greeks in a town which included merchants from all around the Mediterranean. In another sense, however, they could be regarded as incomers since their families are both from Athens rather than from Delos itself. In their images, the couple have an appearance which identifies them with the elites of the Aegean islands and Asia Minor. As well as the more obvious statements made through the inscription and the appearance of the statues themselves, however, there are more subtle messages expressed through the architectural syntax of the part of the house in which the statue group is located. The monument's position opposite the street door superficially appears to cater to a conception of the boundaries of the house as relatively permeable and open to the exterior gaze. In reality, however, there is almost no view of the interior except that of the images themselves, suggesting that the permeability is in fact illusory. A single component of the domestic environment can therefore convey a variety of different and even conflicting messages about a single aspect of identity, namely cultural affiliation.

A further issue here is intentionality: while the images of Cleopatra and Dioscorides, or indeed the Dominus Julius mosaic, can perhaps be viewed at some level as direct and conscious statements of identity, in other instances the case is less clear. For example, to what extent can the spatial syntax of one of the Delian houses be read as expressing cultural affiliation rather than more directly as a means of supporting a set of culturally specific patterns of behaviour? Or how far can the provision of a decorated andron be seen as a statement of wealth and status rather than simply as part of an effort to make the room comfortable for its occupants? The answer is perhaps that various readings are and were possible. Different audiences may have attached more or less significance to particular elements of the layout or decoration of a house, drawing conclusions rooted in their own ethnic and cultural backgrounds and their personal status, gender, experience and values. We must therefore recognise that in choosing to single out and interpret specific elements of the domestic environment we are focusing on a few elements and possible readings from a more varied and complex web of meanings.

Finally, there is also the question of whose identity is being expressed. Here again there is no simple answer. Collective identity of the household as a whole is likely to be one aspect, so, for example, by constructing a house which materialises some of the ideals of a particular cultural group (such as those about privacy, discussed above), the occupants may be expressing their membership of that group. But this collective dimension was probably balanced by another representing individual identity. For example, the architecture of the room in which the Dominus Julius mosaic was originally set seems designed to emphasise the personal power and status of the householder by providing a dramatic backdrop against which he could appear to receive visitors. It is possible that a single architectural feature could carry messages about the householder as an individual and about the household as a group: for instance, the Dominus Julius mosaic can be read both as an attempt by the owner of the house in which it lay to position himself within the sphere of culturally Roman elites across the Empire, and also as a more general claim to wealth and prosperity by the household as a whole. Nonetheless, given what the textual sources from the cultural contexts considered here imply about the dominance of elite males and their role in representing their households in the public sphere, attempts to make such fine distinctions should not be pushed too far: the male householder may frequently have stood as a symbol of the household as a whole.

There are thus a range of major issues and themes which can be addressed by juxtaposing the different case studies included in this volume. At the same time, however, the diversity of cultural norms this reveals, along with the heterogeneous character of the evidence, emphasises some important points about how domestic material can and should be approached. No single set of techniques and questions can be applied uniformly across the ancient world to analyse the archaeological evidence of housing: the variety, not only in the domestic structures themselves but also in the underlying social systems by which those structures were shaped, means that domestic evidence is appropriate for addressing a specific range of questions in any one cultural context. At the same time methodologies also need to be used selectively in order to take account of the quantity and character of the archaeological material and to make the most of the evidence available. For example, exploration of spatial syntax in a large sample of houses is revealing in the Greek Early Iron Age context, where the full plans of numerous houses are available for study, while at Pompeii detailed analysis of artefacts offers a means of exploring patterns of activity within individual households.

The range of analytical strategies at our disposal is far from static, and future work can be anticipated in a variety of important areas. From the theoretical perspective, as I have argued in relation to Pompeii, the formulation of increasingly sophisticated models will enable us to overcome some of the difficulties currently involved in interpreting finds assemblages. This process will inevitably also lead to modifications of data-collection practices in the field. More detailed information about the stratigraphic and spatial locations of artefacts will enable increasingly reliable assessment of the kinds of contexts in which they were excavated and of the patterns of behaviour which they may signal. At the same time the range of questions which can be addressed can be increased by paying attention to information which has not traditionally been gathered. This will include more systematic study of environmental remains such as bones and seeds, which at a basic level reveal patterns of food storage and consumption, but which can also be used to address more complex issues such as ways in which cultural contact affected eating and drinking habits.

Future work should also continue to investigate a range of different social groups. Many of the structures I have discussed in this volume probably belonged to wealthier households. There are a number of reasons for this: such houses tend to be larger and incorporate more rooms, so that spatial organisation is more complex and potentially more revealing. At the same time their owners had sufficient resources to invest in architectural elaboration and in larger numbers of artefacts, some of which remain to be discovered by archaeologists. Features such as mosaics and wall paintings, which are more abundant in larger structures, were also, in the past, what tended to draw the attention of archaeologists and lead to excavation. Despite these biases, however, we have seen in relation to Early Iron Age Greece, in Pompeii and on Delos that in some contexts it is still possible to explore ways in which social and cultural life intersect with socio-economic status. It is to be hoped that more intensive investigation of the less abundant archaeological traces left by less well-off households will yield new insights, as household archaeology rightly assumes a role as one of the numerous established subfields of classical archaeology.

The question of analytical strategies also raises a larger issue. As I pointed out in the Introduction to this volume, scholars' interpretations of ancient domestic material have often tended to be shaped by their readings of texts. Work has focused, for example, on searching for archaeological evidence which supports literary depictions of the reception of visitors at a symposium or *salutatio*. As we have seen, such studies have offered important insights into the use of domestic space in different cultural contexts. At the same time, however, it is important to recognise that there is also potential for exploration beyond and outside where the texts lead, for instance investigating the activities of individuals whose viewpoints do not appear prominently in texts and images, such as slaves in the households of Pompeii or the occupants of the smaller houses on Delos. In suggesting that we should depart further from the texts I may seem to be implying that the disciplines of 'ancient history' and 'classical archaeology' should move further apart, but that is not my intention. It is true that the two fields sometimes have different ways of framing questions and that each has its own strengths and weaknesses. Classical archaeology has often been seen as providing particular insight into questions relating to a medium timeframe of decades or generations, but considered weaker as a means of studying short-term, daily, events or long-term change over centuries (Snodgrass 1991). Nevertheless, what we are dealing with is a spectrum of timeframes, and much of the evidence archaeologists recover results from the actions of individuals. While their precise identities cannot usually be determined, we can still begin to associate those actions with members of specific social groups, some of whose other activities can be studied using textual sources. In doing so, we can aim to work towards a dialogue, bridging – in the domestic context – between archaeologists' discussions of 'households' and historians' discussions of 'families'.

Glossary

The following represents an attempt to define briefly some of the more technical words used in this book which may be unfamiliar to the general reader. In my text I have tried to explain each one where it first appears, and have included words on the following list either for reference if they appear more than once, or if they are used in captions and cannot conveniently be explained there. Both singular and plural are listed below if both appear in the book, otherwise only the form used here is given.

Andron (pl. andrones): Greek term often translated literally as 'men's room'. The precise range of uses to which this space was put is unclear, but it does seem to have been a space in which symposia could be held. As such it can be identified archaeologically by a distinctive configuration of off-set doorway and plain or raised border on the floor, both of which accommodated couches. In addition there was often mosaic and/or painted decoration and sometimes also an anteroom. (See Plate 3.1.)

Atrium (pl. atria): Latin term generally interpreted as designating the large central hall with central roof opening, found in Roman houses in Campania and elsewhere. (See Figures 5.1, 5.2 and 5.3 and Plate 5.1.)

Axiality: apparent central view created lengthwise through a space or building. (See Figure 4.7.)

Cena: Latin term for a formal dinner or banquet.

Clientes (sing. *cliens*): Latin term loosely translated here as 'client', indicating individuals who rely on the help of a *patronus* or 'patron' to promote their interests and undertake services in return.

Compluvium: an opening in the roof of the atrium of a Campanian house, functioning to let in light, air and, on occasion, rainwater, which ran into a central pool or impluvium and was collected in cistern beneath, for household use. (See Plate 5.1.)

Cryptoporticus: Latin term designating a covered walkway.

Dado: painted or moulded strip running along a wall.

Dipinto (pl. dipinti): Italian term referring to painted lettering.

Dolium (pl. dolia): Latin term describing a large storage jar.

Dominus: Latin term referring to the master of a household.

Domus (pl. *domus*): Latin term with a range of meanings from the physical house through to the household occupying that house.

Emblema (pl. emblemata): central figured panel in a mosaic floor.

Fauces: literally 'throat'. Latin term for the narrow entrance corridor of a Roman house. (See Figures 5.1, 5.2 and 5.3.)

Frieze: narrow band of decoration.

Insula (pl. insulae): literally 'island'. Latin term used by scholars to indicate a building block in an urban setting.

Koine: Greek term designating an area of shared culture.

Nilotic: style of decoration featuring water scenes with elements such as papyrus plants and ducks, inspired by depictions of the river Nile in Egypt. (See Plate 6.3.)

Nymphaeum: Latin term referring to a fountain or water feature.

Oikos: Greek term, usually meaning household.

Pastas: Greek term used by modern scholars to describe a form of portico giving off the courtyard of a house and providing access to several rooms. (See Figure 3.1.)

Pater familias: Latin term referring to the master of the house.

Peristyle: courtyard with colonnade running around all four sides. (See Figures 4.1 and 5.3.)

Polis: Greek term meaning 'city' or, more specifically, 'citizen state'.

Salutatio: Latin term referring to an occasion on which a patron would formally receive clients at his home.

Stibadium: Latin term used to designate a curved couch on which a number of diners would recline. (See Figure 6.1.)

Symposium: Greek term indicating a drinking party exclusively for men (although unrelated female entertainers may have been present).

Tablinum: Latin term used by modern scholars to indicate a space lying between the atrium and peristyle or garden in a canonical atrium house. (See Figure 5.3.)

Tesselated: made up of small cubes or tesserae.

Tessera (pl. tesserae): Latin term describing small cubes (usually of stone) used to compose a mosaic.

Triclinium: literally 'three-couch room'. Latin term for a dining room furnished with couches on which diners could recline.

Period names and dates referred to in this book

c. 1100–700 BCE	Early Iron Age in Greece
c. 700–480 BCE	Archaic period in Greece
480–323 BCE	Classical period in Greece
323–31 BCE	Hellenistic period in Greece
509–31 BCE	Roman Republic
Mid 2nd century BCE	Roman conquests of Greece and Africa
31 BCE–476 CE	Roman Empire
79 CE	Destruction of Pompeii
c. 380–400 CE	Dominus Julius mosaic laid

Bibliographic essay

Research on Greek and Roman housing carried out before the 1980s consists largely of descriptions and reconstructions of dwellings based upon archaeological and textual sources. Most publications take the form of excavation reports discussing architecture (sometimes taking different aspects such as wall paintings or mosaic floors in isolation) and often also listing separately some of the pottery and small objects found during excavation. (One example is the preliminary publication of Francis Kelsey's work at Karanis: Boak and Peterson 1931, Husselman 1979. Others are listed below in connection with the case studies presented in the different chapters.) These reports of the primary evidence were supplemented by a small number of more summary works which sought to provide overviews of the material, drawing out general patterns in house-form across space and time, such as Rider 1916, McKay 1975, Graham 1966. While such studies continue to appear (for example Ellis 2000, Gros 2001), scholars have also now directed their attention to achieving a more holistic understanding of the roles played by houses in their wider cultural settings, with particularly intensive study devoted to issues raised by ancient authors.

There has been a marked difference between work on Greek and on Roman contexts in terms of the issues which have been addressed. In relation to Roman housing a number of scholars have discussed in detail the way in which wealthy householders used their dwellings to demonstrate their power and status, a major aspect of elite housing which is emphasised by the first-century BCE architect Vitruvius (for instance Clarke 1991; Wallace-Hadrill 1994; Zanker 1998; Trümper 1998; Hales 2003; Leach 2004). In Greek contexts, much attention has been directed towards investigating whether domestic space was divided into male and female areas, as seems to be implied by the few surviving textual accounts of Athenian domestic arrangements in the fourth century BCE, and also by Vitruvius' comments on Greek houses (for example Walker 1983 [reprinted 1993]; Raeder 1988; Reber 1988; Jameson 1990; Karadedos 1990; Nevett 1994; Goldberg 1999; Antonaccio 2000). More recently, however, scholarship has branched out to consider other questions. These include changes through time in the types of houses constructed and their associated patterns of social relationships; and the role of the domestic sphere in the economy and broader society (for example Cahill 2002 and the

153

papers included in Ault and Nevett 2005; Westgate, Fisher and Whitley 2007 and Vogeikoff-Brogan and Glowacki, in press).

These studies have led to valuable insights into the lives of the households once occupying the excavated structures, revealing some of the ways in which the architecture of ancient houses reinforced certain patterns of social life. At the same time such work has also made clear some of the limitations of the ancient texts, showing, for instance, that the Roman world comprised dwellings with a great variety of different scales, patterns of architecture and quantities and styles of decoration, only some of which can have showcased the power and status of their owners in this manner (for example Pirson 1999). It has also revealed that space in Greek houses was influenced by a variety of social and cultural factors besides gender (Nevett 1999, 68–74). These findings make us challenge some of our assumptions about how ancient households worked and force us to reflect on our interpretations of the texts, emphasising that our surviving written sources present, at best, a partial and sometimes distorted view which is biased towards the geographical and social perspectives of a limited group of individuals. A few scholars have sought to move beyond the agenda set by written sources, tackling instead issues arising directly from the archaeological material itself. This kind of work has provided new insights into ancient households: for example, in Roman contexts it has demonstrated that the atria in high-status houses were also used for storage and for domestic activities such as weaving and cooking (Allison 2004).

As is highlighted in the quotations prefacing the individual chapters, my approach to this material has been both informed by the ancient texts and also strongly influenced by studies of housing undertaken by scholars working in other disciplines (discussed in Nevett 1999, 29-33), and I continue to be inspired by, for example, work done on space syntax (Hanson 1998; Space Syntax, various dates).

CHAPTER 2

The 'rise of the polis' is a topic which has attracted much discussion. Contrasting perspectives and differing conclusions are presented, for example, by Anthony Snodgrass, who suggests that it resulted from rapid social change over a relatively short period during the eighth century (Snodgrass 1980); Lin Foxhall, who argues that social complexity was in fact present throughout this period (Foxhall 1995); and Ian Morris and Sarah Morris, each of whom independently infers a much longer, slower, process of social change (respectively, I. Morris 2000, and S. Morris 1992). Several comprehensive studies have greatly simplified the task of trying to understand developments in Greek Early Iron Age housing, namely: Fagerström 1988b; Lang 1996; Mazarakis Ainian 1997; Morris 1998).

Among the many sites which have yielded domestic material relevant to this chapter, some of the best-preserved buildings recorded in the most detail are Unit IV.I from Nichoria (originally published in Coulson 1983, with revised interpretations offered by Fagerström 1988a and by Mazarakis Ainian 1992) and the houses from Zagora (Cambitoglou *et al.* 1971; Cambitoglou *et al.* 1988). The latter structures have been discussed particularly frequently, serving as a basis for inferences about social life: Ian Morris has used them to argue that patterns of domestic social relations characteristic of the Classical polis can be can be traced back to the eighth century and others have subsequently supported his view (Morris 1999, Morris 2000, 280–286; see also Coucouzeli 2007). Even if Morris is right, however, the houses from Zagora are, as far as we know, unique and, I would argue, cannot be taken as representative of patterns of house-form and social relations during the eighth century BCE.

The possible association between the Classical form of house and patterns of domestic social life linked with citizen status is touched on again in Chapter 3. The case is argued in more detail in Nevett 1999, esp. 156–157 and Nevett 2009a; see also Westgate 2007.

CHAPTER 3

For a comprehensive discussion of various avenues of research on symposia, with further references, see Murray 2003. On drinking parties in the public sphere see Steiner 2002, also with further references. Social drinking has been the subject of extensive work in other cultural contexts, including the Late Bronze Age Aegean: see, for example, Wright 2004. For reclining banquets in the Near East see, for example, Dentzer 1982.

A summary of the arguments for and against female segregation within Classical households is presented by Nicholas Cahill in connection with the evidence from Olynthus: Cahill 2002. The organisation of Classical Greek courtyard houses both at Olynthus and more generally, together with its possible social significance, is explored in Nevett 1999, *passim*, where the term 'single-entrance, courtyard house' is used to describe houses like those from Olynthus, discussed here. The excavations at Olynthus were directed and published by David Robinson: Robinson 1929–1952.

The extent to which ceramic iconography can be used to understand ancient patterns of thought and behaviour has been extensively debated; see, for example, Ferrari 2002, 17–25. There is also a large literature on the iconography of drinking: see, for instance, Lissarrague 1990a, Lissarrague 1990b; Schmitt-Pantel 1992; Lissarrague 1994; Schäfer 1997; Osborne 2007. Thalia Sini specifically discusses the representation of architectural space where drinkers are combined with columns: Sini 1997. The significance of images of symposia in which the participants apparently recline on the ground is examined in detail by Kathryn Topper (Topper 2009). The introduction of these scenes in the late sixth century BCE is interpreted by Alfred Schäfer as evidence that during this period symposia were relocated from enclosed androns to open exterior spaces. He argues that this shift was linked with broadening participation in symposium culture (Schäfer 1997, 41–42). Nevertheless, not only (as I argue here) can it not be demonstrated that social drinking took place in houses in a specialised room at such an early date, but also it is not certain that changes in the iconography can be related so directly to alterations in social practice. The use of domestic courtyard spaces for drinking has been explored, in addition, by Kathleen Lynch (Lynch 2007, 244–246).

My account here of the developing architectural context for the symposium runs counter to some other interpretations which have viewed the formal andron as an architectural space emerging much earlier in Greek houses (for example Hoepfner 1999, 141–148). In his recent detailed re-examination of textual, iconographic and archaeological evidence for a variety of forms of social drinking in the Archaic Greek world, Adam Rabinowitz has similarly concluded that during that period the symposium was firmly located in the public, rather than in the domestic, sphere (Rabinowitz, forthcoming).

CHAPTER 4

The houses of Delos have been one focus for French archaeologists associated with the French School at Athens. Their work is published in the series *Exploration archéologique de Délos faite par l'Ecole Française d'Athènes* (EAD) and in the journal *Bulletin de Correspondance Hellénique* (BCH). Delos has often been excluded from studies of both Greek and Roman housing: in the context of studies of Classical and Hellenistic evidence such as Nevett 1999 their date is relatively late, and for discussion of Roman housing such as Ellis 2000 they are relatively early. A partial exception to this general picture is Tang 2005, in which the evidence of housing on Delos is compared with that of the Roman provincial settlements at Carthage and Ampurias.

An invaluable study and catalogue of the houses on Delos has been produced by Monika Trümper (Trümper 1998), who has also written a series of stimulating articles on individual aspects of housing and domestic social life on the island (Trümper 2003b, Trümper 2004, Trümper 2005b, Trümper 2007). A selection of houses are also discussed by Nicholas Rauh (Rauh 1993), whose conclusions about the social status of the occupants are somewhat controversial. Precise, absolute dating of the individual structures is difficult. Based on her thorough re-examination of the architectural evidence on site, Trümper has been able to suggest relative chronologies for the construction and modification of individual buildings (see Trümper 1998, 120–126 for general discussion and her Catalogue for individual houses, supplemented by Trümper 2002 for the Theatre Quarter). Where deep soundings have been carried out the results have been difficult to interpret (on work in insula III of the Theatre Quarter compare Brun and Brunet 1997 with Trümper 2003a). The third-century date for the original construction of the House of Cleopatra and Dioscorides is that given in the earlier literature (see Trümper 1998, 273–274 for references). Assessing the date of abandonment of the houses is difficult although it seems likely that, once the city had begun to decline, major renovation projects of houses would rapidly have ceased, so that the final phases of the individual properties can be considered roughly contemporary with each other even if the buildings themselves were originally constructed at different times.

The houses analysed here are a subset of the group Trümper discusses in her monograph (Trümper 1998). For the pose and dress of the figures of Cleopatra and Dioscorides see Stewart 1990, 227. The architecture of the house and the location of the monument are discussed in detail by Martin Kreeb (Kreeb 1985b, Kreeb

1988, 17–21; the latter work also explores the use of sculpture in Delian houses more generally). Although some of the small finds from domestic buildings on Delos have been published (Deonna 1938), the contents of individual houses and insulae have not generally been studied in context. Some exceptions are the house of the seals (Siebert 2001; also discussed in Trümper 2005a) and the insula of the comedians (Bruneau 1970), although many of the objects recorded in the latter structure relate to a final phase of use when much of the building was occupied by a workshop for manufacturing purple dye. For further discussion of the 'liturgical' paintings and their cultural significance, with references to previous studies, see Nevett 2009b.

The literature on the issue of 'Romanisation' and acculturation in the Roman Empire is vast. Here I have picked up on calls to study how acculturation worked in relation to lower-status individuals by, for example, Sue Alcock, Simon James and Richard Hingley (Alcock 2001; James 2001; Hingley 2005, 92–93), and on appeals to address the formation of new local cultures on a more regional basis by, for instance, David Mattingly (Mattingly 2002). Examples of other studies where the latter has been attempted include the papers in van Dommelen and Terrenato 2007 and the book-length treatments Woolf 1998 and Mattingly 2006. For discussion of the interaction between local cultures in Italy prior to the Imperial period see, for example, Terrenato 2001; and on aspects of the formation of 'Roman' culture MacMullen 2000 and Wallace-Hadrill 2008.

CHAPTER 5

Much of the extensive body of scholarly literature on Pompeian houses appears in Italian or German, including the catalogue of paintings and mosaics (Bragantini 1983) and the series entitled *Häuser in Pompeji*, which contains detailed architectural descriptions, drawings and phased plans of individual houses. An impression of the variety and level of preservation of the finds from the site is given by Ciarallo and de Carolis 2000, the catalogue of an exhibition devoted to the use of natural resources and level of technology at the time of the destruction. Wooden furniture preserved at Pompeii's neighbour, Herculaneum, is discussed in detail by Mols 1999.

Andrew Wallace-Hadrill's original article on the social structure of the Roman house (Wallace-Hadrill 1988) was republished, along with some of his other work on Pompeian housing, in Wallace-Hadrill 1994. Penelope Allison's detailed analysis of a sample of houses together with their finds (Allison 2004) is supplemented by an excellent website containing further discussion of the individual structures together with a searchable database of the rooms and finds from each one (Allison, date unknown). A selection of other approaches to Roman domestic space, at Pompeii and elsewhere, can be found in Laurence and Wallace-Hadrill 1997.

All of the houses discussed here were studied by Allison. In addition, the House of the Ceii is published in full in the *Häuser in Pompeji* series (Michel 1990). Publication of the insula of the Menander, including the house itself and its finds, was carried out under the editorship of Roger Ling (see Ling 1997; Painter 2001;

Ling and Ling 2005; Allison 2006). At the time this chapter was written the volume on the finds, by Penelope Allison, had not yet appeared but descriptions of a selection of the best-preserved items, together with high quality photographs and brief discussion, were available in an exhibition catalogue (Stefani 2003a). House vi.16.26 has been published only in preliminary form and without discussion of dating and phasing (Sogliano 1908, 183–192).

CHAPTER 6

Roman houses have been excavated in the North African cities in overwhelming numbers. For an extensive, though not up-to-date, catalogue of complete, excavated, structures see Rebuffat 1969 and Rebuffat 1974. A classic study of the social significance of the architecture of Roman houses in North Africa by Yvon Thébert appeared in English in 1987 (Thébert 1987). More recently a variety of aspects of Roman housing in modern Tunisia have been discussed in Bullo and Ghedini 2003 and Carucci 2008. For housing in the Late Roman period more generally see Lavan *et al.* 2007, which includes extensive bibliographic essays.

The large numbers of mosaics found in the North African houses have been the subject of much discussion. In 1910 Paul Gauckler published a scholarly catalogue of some of the first to be found, including many of those mentioned here (although not the Dominus Julius mosaic, which came to light later): Gauckler 1910. For more recent treatment see Dunbabin 1978 and Dunbabin 1999, 101–129, with further references. Numerous popular books have featured mosaics from Tunisia and elsewhere in North Africa, including the Dominus Julius mosaic; for examples see Slim 1995 and Ennaïfer 1996.

The circumstances of the discovery of the Dominus Julius mosaic are reported only briefly by its excavator, Alfred Merlin (Merlin 1921, esp. 96 n. 2, which offers the only description of its architectural context). Its date is discussed by Katherine Dunbabin (Dunbabin 1978, 252, Dunbabin 1999, 118), and the relationship between this and season mosaics generally is treated, for example, in Dunbabin 1978, 252; Parrish 1979, Parrish 1984, 55–56. The symbolic significance of apsidal rooms is explored by, for example, Bek 1983 and Ellis 1991, esp. 122.

The architectural setting of the Dominus Julius mosaic has not tended to be discussed, so I offer here some references to work on other structures, on which my reconstruction of the room (Figure 6.1) is based. Merlin reported that by the time of his excavation the perimeter wall of the room's apse did not survive above about a metre in height, but there are better-preserved parallels in dining rooms elsewhere in the Roman world for various aspects of the arrangements he describes. A well-preserved masonry stibadium in an aristocratic house at Faragola (Perugia, Italy) incorporates evidence for a fountain in front of the couch (Dal Maso 2005), and such an arrangement is also known from a few other published examples (see Morvillez 1996, 129–130). The feature Merlin describes around the perimeter of the apse of the Dominus Julius room seems to have been a raised basin 0.4 m in width with mosaic on the bottom. A well-preserved fourth-century CE masonry stibadium from a villa in Cordoba (Spain) was located in a square (rather than apsidal) room, which had a nymphaeum on the back wall feeding a fountain at the centre of the stibadium (Vaquerizo and Noguera 1997, 60–79). The overall effect may have been similar to (albeit on a smaller scale than) the exedra in the Canopus complex of Hadrian's villa at Tivoli (see Salza Prina Ricotti 1985, 175–176, who also offers a detailed discussion of a variety of examples of triclinia in which water features played a major role, both excavated and from textual descriptions).

The symbolism of the dining practices of Roman elites is discussed at length by Katherine Dunbabin: Dunbabin 2003, who has also compared Roman and Greek customs: Dunbabin 1998. For dining in provincial contexts during the Late Roman period in particular see, for example, the work of Simon Ellis, especially Ellis 1991, Ellis 1997b.

On the Zliten mosaics see Aurigemma 1926, 97 and Dunbabin 1978, 278. For the dates of the Zliten and Oudna mosaics, and earlier references, see Dunbabin 1978, 235–237 and 265–266, respectively. The issue of viewership in relation to the mosaics, paintings and other art works of the Roman world has attracted a variety of recent discussion: see, for example, Clarke 2003; Elsner 2007. Some of the complexities involved in the use of Roman art from domestic contexts to express status and identity are explored in Stewart 2008, Chapter 2. For recent treatments of the archaeological survey evidence which serves as a background to my discussion of the agricultural context of the mosaics see Leone and Mattingly 2004 and Stone 2004 (although neither would necessarily agree with my interpretation of the current evidence). In parallel with my argument presented here, Simon Ellis has suggested that the many bucolic scenes appearing in mosaics from houses in the Greek East are also inspired more by contemporary elite ideology than by the existence of large numbers of elite country villas in that part of the Empire: Ellis 1997a, 39 and 45–46.

Bibliography

Åkerström-Hougen, G. (1974) *The Calendar and Hunting Mosaics of the Villa of the Falconer in Argos*. Stockholm (Acta Instituti Atheniensis Regni Sueciae, Series 4 22)

Akurgal, E. (1983) *Alt-Smyrna* I. *Wohnschichten und Athena-tempel*. Ankara

Alcock, S. (2001) 'Vulgar Romanization and the Dominance of Elites', in S. Keay and N. Terrenato, eds., *Italy and the West: comparative issues in Romanization*, 227–230. Oxford

Allison, P. (2004) *Pompeian Households*. Los Angeles

(2006) *The Insula of the Menander at Pompeii:* III. *The Finds, a Contextual Study*. Oxford

(date unknown) 'Pompeian Households', available at: http://www.stoa. org/projects/ph/home, accessed 15 May 2006

Antonaccio, C. (2000) 'Architecture and behavior: building gender into Greek houses', *Classical World* 93: 517–533

Ault, B. A. and Nevett, L. C. (2005) *Ancient Greek Houses and Households: chronological, regional and social diversity*. Philadelphia

Aurigemma, S. (1926) *I mosaici di Zliten*. Rome

(1962) *L'Italia in Africa. Le scoperte archeologiche: Tripolitania* I. *I monumenti d'arte decorativa. Part* II. *Le pitture d'età romana*. Rome

Barker, G. (1979) 'Economic life at Berenice', in J. A. Lloyd, ed., *Excavations at Sidi Khrebish Benghazi (Berenice)*, 1–49. Tripoli

Bek, L. (1983) '*Quaestiones conviviales*: the idea of the triclinium and the staging of convivial ceremony from Rome to Byzantium', *Analecta Romana Instituti Danici* 12: 81–107

Berry, J. (1997) 'Household artefacts: towards a re-interpretation of Roman domestic space', in Laurence and Wallace-Hadrill 1997, 183–195

Bezerra de Meneses, U. and Sarian, H. (1973) 'Nouvelles peintures liturgiques de Délos', in *Etudes Déliennes (Bulletin de Correspondance Hellénique Supplement* I*)*, 77–109

Bingen, J. (1967) 'L'établissement géométrique et la nécropole ouest', in J. Bingen H. Mussche, J. de Geyter, G. Donnay and T. Haekens, eds., *Thorikos 1964*, 1–56. Brussels

Boak, A. E. R. and Peterson, E. E. (1931) *Karanis 1924–8*. Ann Arbor

Boersma, J. (2000) 'Peisistratos' building activity reconsidered', in H. Sancisi-Weerdenburg, ed., *Peisistratos and the Tyranny: a reappraisal of the evidence*, 49–56. Amsterdam

Bonini, P. (2006) *La casa nella Grecia romana: forme e funzioni dello spazio privato fra I e VI secolo*. Perugia

Bradley, K. (1991) *Discovering the Roman Family: studies in Roman social history.* Oxford

Bragantini, I. ed. (1983) *Pitture e pavimenti di Pompei.* Rome

Brooks, R. (1982) 'Events in the archaeological context and archaeological explanation', *Current Anthropology* 23: 67–75

Brun, P. and Brunet, M. (1997) 'Une huilerie du premier siècle avant J.-C. dans le quartier du théâtre à Délos', *Bulletin de Correspondance Hellénique* 121: 573–615

Bruneau, P. *et al.* (1970) *L'Îlot de la maison des comédiens.* Paris (Exploration archéologique de Délos 27)

Bruno, V. J. (1985) *Hellenistic Painting Techniques: the evidence of the Delos fragments.* Leiden

Bullo, S. and Ghedini, F. eds. (2003) *Amplissimae atque ornatissimae domus.* Rome

Cahill, N. D. (2002) *Household and City Organization at Olynthus.* New Haven

Cambitoglou, A., Birchall, A., Coulton, J. and Green, J. R. (1988) *Zagora II. Excavation of a Geometric Town.* Athens

Cambitoglou, A., Coulton, J. J., Birmingham, J. and Green, J. R. (1971) *Zagora I. Excavation Season 1967, Study Season 1968–9.* Sydney

Cartledge, P. (2002) *The Greeks: a portrait of self and others.* Oxford

Carucci, M. (2008) *The Romano-African Domus: studies in space, decoration and function.* Oxford

Ciarallo, A. and De Carolis, E. eds. (2000) *Homo Faber: Pompeii – life in a Roman town.* Milan

Clarke, J. R. (1991) *The Houses of Roman Italy, 100 BC–AD 250: ritual, space and decoration.* Berkeley

(2003) *Art in the Lives of Ordinary Romans.* Berkeley

Coldstream, J. N. (1977) *Geometric Greece.* London

Cooley, A. and Cooley, M. G. L. (2004) *Pompeii: a sourcebook.* London

Coucouzeli, A. (1998) 'Architecture, power, and ideology in Dark Age Greece: a new interpretation of the Lefkandi Toumba building', in R. Docter and E. Moormann, eds., *Proceedings of the XV International Congress of Classical Archaeology, Amsterdam July 12–17*, 126–129. Amsterdam

(2007) 'Architecture and social structure in early Iron Age Greece', in Westgate, Fisher and Whitley 2007, 169–182

Coulson, W. (1983) 'The architecture: area IV', in W. Coulson, J. Rosser and W. McDonald, eds., *Excavations at Nichoria in Southwest Greece*, 18–56. Minneapolis

Coulson, W., Haggis, D., Mook, M. and Tobin, J. (1997) 'Excavations on the Kastro at Kavousi: an architectural overview', *Hesperia* 66: 317–390

Curtis, R. I. (1984) 'A personalized floor mosaic from Pompeii', *American Journal of Archaeology* 88: 557–566

Dal Maso, C. (2005) 'Torna alla luce una mensa gioiello "E' come quella dell'Ultima Cena"', *La Repubblica*, available at: http://www.repubblica.it/2005/h/sezioni/spettacoli_e_cultura/scavipu/scavipu/scavipu.html

Deetz, J. (1977) *In Small Things Forgotten*. New York

Dentzer, J.-M. (1982) *Le motif du banquet couché dans le Proche-Orient et le monde grec du VIIe au IVe siècle avant J.-C.* Rome

Deonna, W. (1938) *Le mobilier délien*. Paris (Exploration archéologique de Délos 18)

Dunbabin, K. (1978) *The Mosaics of Roman North Africa*. Oxford
  (1998) '*Ut Graeco more biberetur*: Greeks and Romans on the dining couch', in I. Nielsen and H. Sigismund Nielsen, eds., *Meals in a Social Context*, 81–101. Aarhus (Aarhus Studies in Mediterranean Antiquity 1)
  (1999) *Mosaics of the Greek and Roman World*. Cambridge
  (2003) *The Roman Banquet: images of conviviality*. Cambridge

Duval, N. (1986) 'L'iconographie des "villas africaines" et la vie rurale dans l'Afrique romaine de l'antiquité tardive', in *Histoire et archéologie de l'Afrique du Nord: actes du IIIe colloque international*, 163–174. Paris

Ellis, S. (1991) 'Power, architecture and decor: how a late Roman aristocrat appeared to his guests', in E. Gazda, ed., *Roman Art in the Private Sphere*, 117–134. Ann Arbor
  (1997a) 'Late antique houses in Asia Minor', in S. Isager and B. Poulsen, eds., *Patron and Pavements in Late Antiquity*, 38–50. Odense
  (1997b) 'Late antique dining: architecture, furnishings, and behaviour', in Laurence and Wallace-Hadrill 1997, 41–52
  (2000) *Roman Housing*. London

Elsner, J. (2007) *Roman Eyes*. Princeton

Ennaïfer, M. (1996) 'Life on the great estates', in M. Ennaïfer, M. Blanchard-Lemée, H. Slim and L. Slim, eds., *Mosaics of Roman Africa: floor mosaics from Tunisia*, 167–188. New York

Fagerström, K. (1988a) 'Finds, function and plan: a contribution to the interpretation of Iron Age Nichoria in Messenia', *Opuscula Atheniensia* 17: 33–50
  (1988b) *Greek Iron Age Architecture*. Göteborg

Fergola, L. (2003) 'Il vasellame fittile', in G. Stefani, ed., *Menander: la casa del Menandro di Pompei*, 162–167. Milan

Ferrari, G. (2002) *Figures of Speech: men and maidens in ancient Greece*. Chicago

Flannery, K. (1972) 'The origins of the village as a settlement type in Mesoamerica and the Near East: a comparative study', in R. Tringham, G. W. Dimbleby and P. J. Ucko, ed., *Man, Settlement and Urbanism*, 23–54. London

Flower, H. I. (1995) *Ancestor Masks and Aristocratic Power in Roman Culture*. Oxford

Foss, P. (1997) 'Watchful Lares: Roman household organization and the rituals of cooking and eating', in Laurence and Wallace-Hadrill 1997, 196–218

Foxhall, L. (1995) 'Bronze to iron: agricultural systems and political structures in Late Bronze Age and Early Iron Age Greece', *Annual of the British School at Athens* 90: 239–250

(2000) 'The running sands of time', *World Archaeology* 31: 484–498

Fusaro, D. (1982) 'Note di architettura domestica greca nel periodo tardo-geometrico e arcaico', *Dialoghi di Archeologia* N.S. 4: 5–30

Gauckler, P. (1910) *Afrique Proconsulaire (Tunisie)*. Paris (Inventaire des Mosaïques de la Gaule et de l'Afrique II)

George, M. (1997) 'Servus and domus: the slave in the Roman house', in Laurence and Wallace-Hadrill 1997, 15–24

Ghiotto, A. R. (2003) 'Le fontane e le vasche ornamentali', in Bullo and Ghedini 2003, 235–247

Gilchrist, R. (2000) 'Archaeological biographies: realizing human life-cycles, -courses and -histories', *World Archaeology* 31: 325–328

Giros, A. (2000) 'Habitudes alimentaires grecques et romaines à Délos à l'époque hellénistique: le témoinage de la céramique', *Pallas* 52: 209–220

Goldberg, M. (1999) 'Spatial and behavioural negotiation in Classical Athenian city houses', in P. Allison, ed., *The Archaeology of Household Activities*, 142–161. London

Goodchild, R. (1986) 'Synesius of Cyrene: bishop of Ptolemais', in J. Reynolds, ed., *Libyan Studies: select papers of the late R. G. Goodchild*, 239–253. London

Graham, J. W. (1966) 'The origins and interrelations of the Greek house and the Roman house', *Phoenix* 20: 3–31

Gros, P. (2001) *L'Architecture romaine* II. *Maisons, villas, palais et tombeaux*. Paris

Hales, S. (2003) *The Roman House and Social Identity*. Cambridge

Hall, S. (1996) 'Introduction: who needs identity?', in S. Hall and P. Du Gay, eds., *Questions of Cultural Identity*, 1–17. London

Hanson, J. (1998) *Decoding Homes and Houses*. Cambridge

Hendon, J. (2005) 'The Engendered Household', in S. M. Nelson, ed., *Handbook of Gender Archaeology*, 171–198

Hillier, B. and Hanson, J. (1984) *The Social Logic of Space*. Cambridge

Hingley, R. (2005) *Globalizing Roman culture: unity, diversity and empire*. London

Hoepfner, W. (1999) 'Die Epoche der Griechen: Athen und Attika', in W. Hoepfner, ed., *Geschichte des Wohnens*, 223–260. Ludwigsburg

Humphrey, C. (1988) 'No place like home in anthropology: the neglect of architecture', *Anthropology Today* 4: 16–18

Hunter, V. (1994) *Policing Athens: social control in the Attic lawsuits, 420–320 BC*. Princeton

Husselman, E. M. (1979) *Karanis Excavations of the University of Michigan in Egypt, 1928–1935: topography and architecture*. Ann Arbor

Izzet, V. (2001) 'Putting the house in order: the development of Etruscan domestic architecture', in J. Rasmus Brandt and Lars Karlsson, eds., *From huts to houses: transformations of ancient societies*, 41–69. Stockholm

James, S. (2001) '"Romanization" and the peoples of Britain', in S. Keay and N. Terrenato, eds., *Italy and the West: comparative issues in Romanization*, 187–209. Oxford

Jameson, M. H. (1990) 'Private space and the Greek city', in O. Murray and S. Price, eds., *The Greek City from Homer to Alexander*, 171–195. Oxford

Jones, C. (1991) 'Dinner Theatre', in W. Slater, ed., *Dining in a Classical Context*, 185–198. Ann Arbor

Jones, J. Ellis, Graham, A. J. and Sackett, L. H. (1973) 'An Attic Country House below the Cave of Pan at Vari', *Annual of the British School at Athens* 68: 355–452

Karadedos, G. (1990) 'Υστεροκλασικό Σπίτι στη Μαρωνεία Θράκης''', *Εγνατία* 2: 265–297

Kent, S. (1991) 'Partitioning space: cross-cultural factors influencing domestic spatial segregation', *Environment and Behaviour* 23: 438–473

Kinch, K. (1914) *Vroulia*. Berlin

Kreeb, M. (1985a) 'Das Delische Wohnhaus', *Archäologische Anzeiger* (1985): 93–111
(1985b) 'Zur Basis der Kleopatra auf Delos', *Horos* 3: 41–61
(1988) *Untersuchungen zur Figürlichen Ausstattung Delischer Privathäuser*. Chicago

Lang, F. (1996) *Archaische Siedlungen in Griechenland: Struktur und Entwicklung*. Berlin

Laurence, R. and Wallace-Hadrill, A. eds. (1997) *Domestic Space in the Roman World: Pompeii and beyond*. Portsmouth, RI

Lavan, L., Özgenel, L. and Sarantis, A. eds. (2007) *Housing in Late Antiquity: from palaces to shops*. Leiden (Late Antique Archaeology 3.2)

Lazer, E. (1997) 'Appendix F: Human skeletal remains in the casa del Menandro room 19', in Ling 1997, 342–343

Leach, E. W. (2004) *The Social Life of Painting in Ancient Rome and on the Bay of Naples*. Cambridge

Leone, A. and Mattingly, D. (2004) 'Vandal, Byzantine and Arab Rural Landscapes in North Africa', in N. Christie, ed., *Landscapes of Change: rural evolutions in Late Antiquity and the Early Middle Ages*, 135–162. Aldershot and Burlington

Ling, R. (1997) *The Insula of the Menander at Pompeii* I. *The Structures*. Oxford

Ling, R. and Clarke, G. (1997) 'Appendix A: Gazetteer', in Ling 1997, 257–324

Ling, R. and Ling, L. (2005) *The Insula of the Menander at Pompeii* II. *The Decorations*. Oxford

Lissarrague, F. (1990a) 'Around the krater: an aspect of banquet imagery', in O. Murray, ed., *Sympotica*, 196–209. Oxford
(1990b) *The Aesthetics of the Greek Banquet: images of wine and ritual*. Princeton
(1994) '*Epiktetos egraphsen*: the writing on the cup', in S. Goldhill and R. Osborne, eds., *Art and Text in Greek Culture*, 12–27. Cambridge

Lynch, K. (2007) 'More thoughts on the space of the symposium', in Westgate, Fisher and Whitley 2007, 243–249

MacKinnon, M. (forthcoming) '"Romanizing" Ancient Carthage: evidence from zooarchaeological remains', in P. Crabtree, D. Campana, S. de France, J. Lev-Tov and A. Choyke, eds., *Anthropological Approaches to Zooarchaeology: colonialism, complexity and animal transformations*. Oxford

MacMullen, R. (2000) *Romanization in the time of Augustus*. New Haven

Maguire, H. (2002) 'The good life', in G. Bowersock, P. Brown and O. Grabar, eds., *Interpreting Late Antiquity*, 238–257. Cambridge, Mass.

Mattingly, D. J. (2002) 'Vulgar and weak "Romanization", or time for a paradigm shift?', *Journal of Roman Archaeology* 15: 536–541

(2006) *An imperial possession: Britain in the Roman Empire, 54 BC–AD 409*. London (The Penguin history of Britain 1)

Mazarakis Ainian, A. (1992) 'Nichoria in the southwestern Peloponnese: units IV-1 and IV-5 reconsidered', *Opuscula Atheniensia* 19: 75–84

(1997) *From Rulers' Dwellings to Temples: architecture, religion and society in Early Iron Age Greece (1100–700 BC)*. Jonsered

(2007) 'Architecture and social structure in Early Iron Age Greece', in Westgate, Fisher and Whitley 2007, 157–168

McKay, A. G. (1975) *Houses, Villas and Palaces in the Roman World*. London

Merlin, M. (1921) 'La mosaïque du seigneur Julius à Carthage', *Bulletin Archéologique* (1921): 95–114

Michel, D. (1990) *Casa dei Cei (1 6 15)*. Munich (Häuser in Pompeji 3)

Miller, D. (2001) 'Behind closed doors', in D. Miller, ed., *Home Possessions: material culture behind closed doors*, 1–19. Oxford

Milnor, K. (2005) *Gender, Domesticity, and the Age of Augustus*. Oxford

Mols, S. (1999) *Wooden Furniture in Herculaneum: form, technique and function*. Amsterdam

Morris, I. (1997) 'Homer and the Iron Age', in I. Morris and B. Powell, eds., *A New Companion to Homer*, 535–559. Leiden

(1998) 'Archaeology and Archaic Greek history', in N. Fisher and H. van Wees, eds., *Archaic Greece: new approaches and new evidence*, 1–91. London

(1999) 'Archaeology and gender ideologies in Early Archaic Greece', *Transactions of the American Philological Association* 129: 305–317

(2000) *Archaeology as Cultural History: words and things in Iron Age Greece*. Oxford

(2005) 'Archaeology, standards of living, and Greek economic history', in J. G. Manning and I. Morris, eds., *The Ancient Economy: evidence and models*, 91–126. Stanford

Morris, S. (1992) 'Introduction: Greece between east and west: perspectives and prospects', in G. Kopcke and I. Tokumaru, eds., *Greece between East and West: tenth to eighth centuries BC*, xiii–xviii. Mainz

Morvillez, E. (1996) 'Sur les installations de lits de table en sigma dans l'architecture domestique du Haut et du Bas-Empire', *Pallas* 44: 119–158

Murray, O. (1983) 'The Greek symposion in history', in E. Gabba, ed., *Tria corda: scritti in onore di Arnaldo Momigliano*, 257–272. Como

(1990) 'Sympotic history', in O. Murray, ed., *Sympotica: a symposium on the symposium*, 3–13. Oxford

(1994) 'Nestor's cup and the origins of the Greek symposion', in B. D'Agostino and D. Ridgway, eds., *Apoikia: scritti in onore di Giorgio Buchner*, 47–54. Naples

(2003) 'Sympotica – twenty years on', *Pallas* 61: 13–21

Nevett, L. C. (1994) 'Separation or seclusion? Towards an archaeological approach to investigating women in the Greek household in the fifth to third centuries BC', in M. Parker Pearson and C. Richards, eds., *Architecture and Order: approaches to social space*, 98–112. London

(1997) 'Perceptions of domestic space in Roman Italy', in B. Rawson and P. Weaver, eds., *The Roman Family in Italy: status, sentiment and space*, 281–298. Oxford

(1999) *House and Society in the Ancient Greek World*. Cambridge

(2002) 'Continuity and change in Greek households under Roman rule: the role of women in the domestic context', in E. Ostenfeld, ed., *Greek Romans or Roman Greeks*, 81–97. Aarhus (Aarhus Studies in Mediterranean Antiquity 3)

(2008) '"Castles in the Air"? The Julius mosaic as evidence for elite country housing in Late Roman North Africa', in A. Mastino, J. Gonzalez and R. Zucca, eds., *Africa Romana. Le ricchezze dell'Africa: risorse, produzioni, scambi*, 745–758. Rome

(2009a) 'Domestic culture in Classical Greece', *Bulletin Antieke Beschaving* Supplement: 59–66

(2009b) 'Domestic facades: a feature of the Greek "urban" landscape?', in S. Owen and L. Preston, eds., *Inside the City in the Greek World*, 118–130. Oxford

(forthcoming) 'Family and household: ancient history and archaeology', in B. Rawson, ed., *A Companion to Families in the Greek and Roman World*. Oxford

Norberg-Schultz, C. (1985) *The Concept of Dwelling*. New York

Osborne, R. (2007) 'Projecting identities in the Greek symposium', in J. Sofaer Derevenski, ed., *Material Identities*, 31–52. Oxford

Pader, E.-J. (1997) 'Domestic routine', in P. Oliver, ed., *Encyclopedia of Vernacular Architecture of the World*, 71–72. Cambridge

Painter, K. (2001) *The Insula of the Menander at Pompeii* IV. *The Silver Treasure*. Oxford

Parrish, D. (1979) 'Two mosaics from Roman Tunisia: an African variation of the season theme', *American Journal of Archaeology* 83: 281–285

(1984) *Season Mosaics of Roman North Africa*. Rome

Pirson, F. (1999) *Mietwohnungen in Pompeji und Herkulaneum*. Munich

Ploumis, I. M. (1997) 'Gifts in the Late Roman iconography', in S. Isager and B. Poulsen, eds., *Patron and Pavements in Late Antiquity*, 125–150. Odense

Preston-Day, L. (1990) 'Early Iron Age architecture at Kavousi', in Πεπραγμένα του ΣΤ' Διέθνους Κρητολογικού Συνεδρίου, 173–183. Chania

Rabinowitz, A. (forthcoming) 'Drinking from the same cup: Sparta and Late Archaic commensality', in S. Hodkinson, ed., *Sparta: comparative approaches*. Swansea

Raeder, J. (1988) 'Vitruv, *de architectura* VI 7 (*aedificia Graecorum*) und die hellenistische Wohnhaus und Palastarchitektur', *Gymnasium 95* 95: 316–368

Rauh, N. K. (1993) *The Sacred Bonds of Commerce*. Amsterdam

Reber, K. (1988) '*Aedificia Graecorum*: zu Vitruvs Beschreibung des griechischen Hauses', *Archäologischer Anzeiger* (1988): 653–666

Rebuffat, R. (1969) 'Maisons à péristyle d'Afrique du nord: répertoire de plans publiés', *Mélanges de l'École française de Rome* 81: 659–724

(1974) 'Maisons à péristyle d'Afrique du nord: répertoire de plans publiés II', *Mélanges de l'École française de Rome* 86: 445–499

Richardson, L. (1988) 'Water triclinia and biclinia in Pompeii', in R. Curtis, ed., *Studia Pompeiana and Classica*, 305–315. New York

Rider, B. C. (1916) *The Greek House: its history and development from the Neolithic period to the Hellenistic age*. Cambridge

Riggsby, A. (1997) '"Public" and "private" in Roman culture: the case of the *cubiculum*', *Journal of Roman Archaeology* 10: 36–56

Robinson, D. M. (1929–1952) *Excavations at Olynthus, Parts I–XIV*. Baltimore

Rossiter, J. J. (1991) 'Convivium and villa in Late Antiquity', in W. Slater, ed., *Dining in a Classical Context*, 199–214. Ann Arbor

Salza Prina Ricotti, E. (1985) 'The importance of water in Roman garden triclinia', in E. B. MacDougall, ed., *Ancient Roman Villa Gardens*, 135–183. Washington

Schäfer, A. (1997) *Unterhaltung beim griechischen Symposion*. Mainz

Schiffer, M. B. (1996) *Formation Processes and the Archaeological Record*. Salt Lake City

Schmitt-Pantel, P. (1990a) 'Sacrificial meal and symposium: two models of civic institutions in the Archaic city', in O. Murray, ed., *Sympotica: a symposium on the symposium*, 14–33. Oxford

(1990b) 'Collective activities and the political in the Greek city', in O. Murray and S. Price, eds., *The Greek City from Homer to Alexander*, 199–214. Oxford

(1992) *La cité au banquet: histoire des repas publics dans les cités grecques*. Rome

Schmitt-Pantel, P. and Tchernia, A. (2004) 'Vin et civilisation', in *Le vin: nectar des dieux, génie des hommes*, 42–55. Gollion

Shaw, B. (1995 [1979]) 'The camel in Roman North Africa and the Sahara: history, biology, and human economy', in *Environment and Society in Roman North Africa* IV, 663–721. Aldershot

Siebert, G. (2001) *L'Îlot des Bijoux, l'îlot des Bronzes, la Maison des Sceaux* I. *Topographie et architecture*. Paris (Exploration archéologique de Délos 38)

Sini, T. (1997) 'A symposion scene on an Attic fourth century calyx-krater in St. Petersburg', in O. Palagia, ed., *Greek Offerings*, 159–165. Oxford

Slim, H. (1995) 'La architettura', in M. Fantar, ed., *I mosaici Romani di Tunisia*, 127–155. Milan

Small, D. (1997) 'City-state dynamics through a Greek lens', in D. L. Nichols and T. H. Charlton, eds., *The Archaeology of City-States: cross-cultural approaches*, 107–118. Washington and London

Smith, T. J. (2000) 'Dancing spaces and dining places: Archaic komasts at the symposion', in G. Tsetskhladze, A. J. N. W. Prag and A. M. Snodgrass, eds.,

Periplous: papers on Classical art and archaeology presented to John Boardman, 309–319. London

Snodgrass, A. M. (1980) *Archaic Greece: the age of experiment.* London, Berkeley and Los Angeles

(1991) 'Structural history and classical archaeology', in J. Bintliff, ed., *The Annales School and Archaeology*, 57–72. Leicester

(2001) *The Dark Age of Greece.*

Sogliano, A. (1908) 'Relazione degli scavi eseguiti dal dicembre 1902 a tutto marzo 1905', *Notizie degli Scavi di Antichità* Series V, 5: 180–192

Space Syntax, *Symposia.* Various dates. Accessed 12/04/10 <http://www.spacesyntax.org/symposia/index.asp#>

Stefani, G. ed. (2003a) *Menander: la casa del Menandro di Pompei.* Milan

(2003b) 'Produzione fittile: attività, consumi, commerci', in Stefani 2003a, 210–223

Steiner, A. (2002) 'Public and private: links between *symposion* and *syssition* in fifth-century Athens', *Classical Antiquity* 21: 347–380

Stewart, A. (1990) *Greek Sculpture: an exploration.* New Haven and London

Stewart, P. (2008) *The Social History of Roman Art.* Cambridge

Stone, D. (2004) 'Problems and possibilities in survey: a North African perspective', in S. Alcock and J. Cherry, eds., *Side-by-side Survey: comparative regional studies in the Mediterranean world*, 132–143. Oxford

Sutton, S. B. (1999) 'Fleeting villages, moving households: Greek housing strategies in historical perspective', in D. Lawrence-Zúñiga and D. Birdwell-Pheasant, ed., *House Life: space, place and family in Europe*, 73–103. Oxford and New York

Tang, B. (2005) *Delos, Carthage, Ampurias.* (Analecta Romana Instituti Danici Supplement 36). Rome

Terrenato, N. (1999) 'The Romanization of Italy: global acculturation or cultural bricolage?', in C. Forcey *et al.*, eds., *Proceedings of the Eighth Annual Theoretical Roman Archaeology Conference*, 20–27. Oxford

(2001) 'Introduction', in S. Keay and N. Terrenato, eds., *Italy and the West: comparative issues in Romanization*, 1–6. Oxford

Thébert, Y. (1987) 'Private life and domestic architecture in Roman Africa', in P. Veyne, ed., *A History of Private Life: from pagan Rome to Byzantium*, 313–409. Cambridge, Mass. and London (English translation by A. Goldhammer)

Topper, K. (2009) 'Primitive life and the construction of the sympotic past in Athenian vase painting', *American Journal of Archaeology* 113: 3–26

Trümper, M. (1998) *Wohnen in Delos: eine baugeschichtliche Untersuchung zum Wandel der Wohnkultur in hellenistischer Zeit.* Rahden (Internationale Archäologie 46)

(2002) 'Das Quartier du théâtre in Delos: Planung, Entwicklung und Parzellierung eines "gewachsenen" Stadtviertels hellenistischer Zeit', *Mitteilungen des deutschen Archäologischen Instituts, Athenischer Abteilung* 117: 133–292

(2003a) 'Ein klassisches Haus in Delos? Zur Chronologie der Maison O in der Insula III des Quartier du théâtre', *Bulletin de Correspondance Hellénique* 127: 139–165

(2003b) 'Material and social environment of Greco-Roman households in the East: the case of Hellenistic Delos', in D. L. Balch and C. Osiek, eds., *Early Christian Families in Context*, 19–43. Grand Rapids, Mich.

(2004) 'Wohnen und arbeiten im hellenistischen Handelshafen Delos', in M. Droste and A. Hoffmann, eds., *Wohnformen und Lebenswelten im interkulturellen Vergleich*, 125–159. Frankfurt

(2005a) 'Die Maison des sceaux in Delos – Ein "versiegelter" Fundkomplex? Untersuchungen zur Aussagekraft und Interpretation der Funde eines durch Brand zerstörten hellenistischen Wohnhauses', *Mitteilungen des Deutschen Archäologischen Instituts, Athenischer Abteilung* 120: 317–416

(2005b) 'Modest housing in Late Hellenistic Delos', in B. A. Ault and L. C. Nevett, eds., *Ancient Greek Houses and Households: chronological, regional, and social diversity*, 119–139. Philadelphia

(2007) 'Differentiation in the Hellenistic houses of Delos: the question of functional areas', in Westgate, Fisher and Whitley 2007, 323–334

van der Veen, M., Grant, A. and Barker, G. (1996) 'Romano-Libyan agriculture: crops and animals', in G. Barker, ed., *Farming the Desert: the UNESCO Libyan Valleys Archaeological Survey* I. Synthesis, 227–263. Tripoli

van Dommelen, P. and Terrenato, N. eds. (2007) *Articulating Local Cultures: power and identity under the expanding Roman republic*. Portsmouth, RI (International Roman Archaeology Conference series 64)

Vanhaverbeke, H., Poblome, J., Vermeulen, F. and Waelkens, M. eds. (2008) *Thinking about Space: the potential of surface survey and contextual analysis in the analysis of space in Roman times*. Leuven (Studies in Eastern Mediterranean Archaeology 8)

Vaquerizo, D. and Noguera, J. M. (1997) *La villa de el Ruedo*. Murcia

Vogeikoff-Brogan, K. and Glowacki, N. eds. (in press) *STEGA: the archaeology of houses and households in Ancient Crete*. Princeton (*Hesperia* Supplement)

Walker, S. (1983 [reprinted 1993]) 'Women and housing in Classical Greece', in A. Cameron and A. Kuhrt, eds., *Images of Women in Classical Antiquity*, 81–91. London

Wallace-Hadrill, A. (1988) 'The social structure of the Roman house', *Proceedings of the British School at Rome* 56: 43–97

(1994) *Houses and Society in Pompeii and Herculaneum*. Princeton

(1996) 'Engendering the Roman house', in D. E. Kleiner and S. B. Matheson, eds., *I Claudia: women in ancient Rome*, 104–115. New Haven

(1998) 'The villa as cultural symbol', in A. Frazer, ed., *The Roman Villa: villa urbana*, 43–53. Philadelphia

(2003) 'Domus and insulae in Rome: families and housefuls', in D. L. Balch and C. Osiek, eds., *Early Christian Families in Context*, 3–18. Grand Rapids, Mich.

(2008) *Rome's Cultural Revolution*. Cambridge

Westgate, R. (2007) 'The Greek house and the ideology of citizenship', *World Archaeology* 39: 229–245

Westgate, R., Fisher, N. and Whitley, J. eds. (2007) *Building Communities: houses, settlement and society in the Aegean and beyond.* London (British School at Athens Studies 15)

Woolf, G. (1998) *Becoming Roman: the origins of provincial civilization in Gaul.* Cambridge

Wright, J. ed. (2004) *The Mycenean Feast* (*Hesperia* Special issue). Princeton

Zanker, P. (1998) *Pompeii: public and private life.* Cambridge, Mass.

Index